BOOKS BY

NAN FAIRBROTHER

The Cheerful Day (1960)

Men and Gardens (1956)

An English Year (1954)

THESE ARE

BORZOI BOOKS,

PUBLISHED IN NEW YORK BY

ALFRED A. KNOPF

THE
CHEERFUL
DAY

For who, to dumb Forgetfulness a prey,
    This pleasing anxious being e'er resign'd,
Left the warm precincts of the cheerful day,
    Nor cast one longing ling'ring look behind?
                GRAY: *"Elegy Written*
                    in a Country Churchyard"

THE
CHEERFUL
DAY

*NAN
FAIRBROTHER*

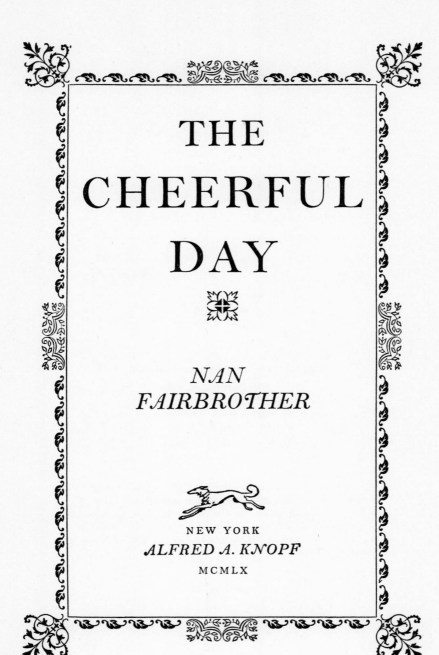

NEW YORK
ALFRED A. KNOPF
MCMLX

L. C. catalog card number: 59–15949

© Nan Fairbrother, 1960

THIS IS A BORZOI BOOK,
PUBLISHED BY ALFRED A. KNOPF, INC.

FIRST EDITION

TO

D. P. AND *J. S.*

WITHOUT WHOSE HELP

THIS BOOK

WOULD NEVER HAVE BEEN WRITTEN

CONTENTS

PART ONE

THE
FIRST
THREE
YEARS
TRANSPLANTED

WE ARE NEW TO LONDON, NEW AND NOT yet at home: a family from the country where the farm was our only neighbour, but now moved suddenly to the centre of an enormous city. We are still half-bewildered by the different element we live in, not yet rooted in our new existence. The London day is beginning, but the day here is strange still, is not yet the familiar pattern we live against, as it will be in time. On the farm we knew by the life outside the windows just where we were in the framework of the day. The cows called in for the morning milking meant the time was just turned six, whether dark at mid-winter or sunny in June. The postman came through the orchard at nine o'clock as near as mattered, the men went off up the field-path for lunch at noon, and the end of our day approaching was the cows coming in again for the evening milking, called in by the cowman at four o'clock. Or if he was late— helping with the threshing in winter perhaps, or hay-making in summer—then we knew without need of clocks exactly how late he was by the growing impatience of the cows herded hopefully round the gate from the meadow.

But nothing here is familiar enough for reference. The life be-

yond our London windows is alien and unmeaning. We are
strangers to its rhythm, living precariously by the clocks and
watches I forget to wind, not peacefully by the farm's reliable
day.

But at least I have wound my watch enough to know that I
must get up now and tell the children it is time for school, two
small boys of six and seven, each in his separate room, sitting up
in bed, playing with toys but very serious, waiting for me to
come—not indeed to wake them, for young children wake always long before we do—but to tell them the time, to get them
ready for school and launch them like ships from the doorstep
into the tumultuous sea of their London day. And because this
new city life is still so strange and swift and alarming, because
they are not yet sure enough to feel at their ease and dawdle, they
get up very quickly, are dressed and downstairs before me always. And when breakfast is over, and satchels packed with
gym-shoes and crayons and notebooks and pencil-boxes—all the
paraphernalia of school—then we set off together up the street
to catch the bus at the top.

To the children newly-come to London this is an astonishing
new universe, bewildering, fascinating, fast and tumultuous beyond anything they imagined could exist. For the background of
their whole lives till now has been the quiet country, with no
traffic, very few people, and if they went with me now and then
to do the shopping in the market, it was an expedition to the
teeming centre of the world. They had never supposed that anywhere could be busier than our local market town.

"We lived on a farm." So Peter began his first essay for his new
London school. I know, because he asked me the spelling for almost every word. "It was a farm, but William is not a farmer. He
is a doctor. William is my father. There were houses. One for the
farmer. The other house for us. Now we came to London. Now
we live in the same house with William. It is the first time we
lived in the same house with William. I think it is very nice."

The First Three Years Transplanted

All their lives till now they lived in the other house, the old forgotten farmhouse across the orchard. They grew up quietly, the three of us together, in a hidden corner, off the main road and down the lane, over the cow-meadow and through the farmyard, across the stream and through the orchard to the old house islanded at last within its moat. No private universe could have been more secure from all outside disturbance, a slow green world of fields and trees and quietly-changing seasons, where we lived all through the war while William was away. So that the children grew up used to silence, more accustomed to animals than people; and their metropolis, the capital city of their native land, was the little near-by market town with its main street blocked with stalls along the roadway. If in their fairy tales "the Prince came at last to a great city," then it was the market square they saw in their imagined scene, crowded with little barrows piled high with apples and potatoes, and under the canvas awnings, rows of brown corduroy trousers and Wellington boots for the winter. And along their great city pavements the country wives went shopping with large country baskets on Saturday mornings, and farmers came to town to sell their cows and stand in the middle of the road to talk to their friends in thick warm country voices.

But now John and Peter live in London, and here all the pavements are crowded with people who hurry always and do not stop to talk; the roads are solid rivers of traffic, implacable, terrifying; and once outside the door the children feel themselves engulfed in this whirlpool, trapped in the bewildering confusion by high unbroken walls of buildings.

It is the traffic above all which troubles them. And no wonder. For on the war-time farm a strange motor-car was a rare and dangerous animal, to be watched and avoided as carefully as the bull in the yard. There were reassuring gates and fences between them, and unless the car was empty they never went too close. As for the traffic on the roads, there was the orchard to cross, the

· 5 ·

yard and the meadow, before they even got as far as the gate into the outside world of motor-cars. And even this main gate opened into a lane so little used that the barriers at the level-crossing of the single-line railway down the road were kept always closed against traffic, and cars must summon the keeper to open the gates before they could pass. Even the main road through the village, the highway of buses and lorries and vans going through to the market, even this all-important thoroughfare of the world was empty enough for our rules of the road to be of the very simplest. "Stay on the pavement," I would tell them when they went by themselves to the village, "and never go on to the road till there's nothing coming from either way for as far as you can see."

It was straightforward advice, confidently given and confidently followed. The way to deal with traffic was very simple they thought—Never go near enough to a motor-car for it to catch you.

And now they must cross Oxford Street.

They stand on the pavement-edge and stare in dismay at the ceaseless torrent of traffic pouring past in front of them from both sides at once. How can they possibly get through alive? How can anyone plunge into a herd of wild animals and hope to reach the other side? If the opposite pavement were at the opposite side of a chasm it would be no more impossible to get there.

"Hold my hands," I say, as they press close in on each side of me. "Keep tight hold and walk across when I do."

I can see that it is truly dreadful to thread their way for the first time between close-packed buses as high as houses, to walk deliberately into this crowd of monsters with no escape or protection. They clutch my hands like drowning men, and I am sure they shut their eyes when we step off the pavement, as they would do walking over a precipice. For it has never occurred to them that motor-cars might be driven by mild reasonable people, quite anxious not to mow down walkers in swathes of dead bodies behind them. Traffic, they think, is dragons, is demons only waiting to catch them off the pavement to chase them and run them down. "To squash us," says John with a certain horrified relish, for John likes his language vivid, and no doubt remembers the poor rolled-out corpses of frogs and hedgehogs he used to examine with sorrow on the country lanes.

"Do you know, Dardy?" Peter told me in amazement, "when we stood still in the middle of the road the traffic went *round* us! Does it often do that in London?"

Crossing Oxford Street to them is like walking into a lions' den with me as the lion-tamer. If I say the lions will not bite, then they believe me since they know I am reliable, but it is an act of faith, and I think they still half-believe that when a car stops and beckons us on, it is not really to let us cross the road, but to get us off the pavement so that it can pounce and catch us.

But already now, after the first few weeks, they grow less fearful, more adventurous. Already when the lights are green they stride confidently across the road in front of the halted herd of monsters. Already John feels a half-fearful delight in walking so close beside a standing car that he can touch it as he passes. I have seen him do it when he thought I did not notice—reach out and give the mud-guard a quick slap, watching the driver as warily as a cat to see what would happen, as if he were teasing a dragon of uncertain temper.

Of course it is disastrous for my reputation. For years there has been all this fuss about not setting foot on the road when a car was in sight, and now I tell them to cross the street with a hundred cars crowding down on them from both sides together. Well, they must learn sometime I suppose, that truth is always relative, and that when they are in Rome they must live like Romans. But still I can imagine them saying to each other when I threaten them with some dreadful warning, "Yes, I know Dardy says so. But you remember what she used to say about traffic when we lived in the country."

Now however, we live in London, and for all of us in this first summer of our arrival there is the new amusement that any change of background gives to the ordinary working day a festival holiday air. I can never see why it should be so, but in a new setting it is always the frivolities we notice, not the serious business of living, but the country inns and cottage gardens, and in the town the gay shop windows, the parks and theatres and people's clothes. No matter what it is we do in the days when we first arrive, the most humdrum occupation takes on a feeling, not of dull routine but of improvising for fun, of amusing ourselves. It is the same for townsfolk new in the country: when they first arrive they feel themselves on holiday and everything a game. They may cook the same meals on inconvenient stoves, or chop up logs and coax a smoky fire to burn so that they can sit and read the same newspaper they have always read. No matter. The dullest tasks all have the air at first of camping out for fun. And I too, new to the town from the homely country shops, set out with a sense of delightful festival to do the same dull household shopping in these sophisticated city streets. Getting up in the morning is like getting up on holiday.

As for the children they are fitfully enchanted. When they are not too dizzy with the strangeness of it all, they find London a hilarious new setting for their lives, intoxicatingly gay after the slow workaday background of the farm routine. Here the coloured traffic whirls by like merry-go-rounds, the humblest journey is an excitement, the streets are all shop windows, and Woolworth's, their favourite shop, is here quite wonderfully transformed from village to metropolis. And then the constant crowds in the streets—these are not serious people going to work, for where are their muddy boots and dirty jackets? These are the world and his wife out walking the pavements in their best clean clothes, and that, so the children think, can never mean work but only holiday.

On the river the boats go up and down for amusement. Even

the sooty barges, John is convinced, are "pleasurey steamers." Tower Bridge (and who could have guessed the grown-up world would hold such glorious toys?) breaks open in the middle and rears up its two separate halves, vertical, astonishing. There are buses going off to a place called Golden Green, so they tell me. They read the name on the front of the bus, they say, and remembered because they liked it. And Golders Green is a suburb suddenly enchanted. In Trafalgar Square their one-armed hero, Nelson, presides as a quite unexpected Master of Ceremonies, high on his column above the whirligig traffic. "In his gold starry coat," they told me, remembering their favourite picture in their history books.

But the enchanted heart of London, the fairyland they never dreamed existed and can still only half believe in, is Piccadilly Circus with all its advertisements lit up at night. What they imagine they are, these glittering cliffs of coloured lights, that I have never been able to find out; but certainly not mere garish reminders of Bovril or somebody's orange squash. Children are mirrors where parents can see the familiar world as if it were newly created.

"Let's go back through the Rocket Square," they plead, no matter where we are. "*Please* let's go and see if the Rocket's still there." The Rocket Square is Piccadilly Circus, and the Rocket itself is a horrible advertisement of cascading coloured lights, too strange and beautiful, they feel, ever to be taken for granted as sober fact. It is an astonishing miracle, not to be relied on, but visited whenever they get the chance, to make sure it is still there. And because true enthusiasm is one of the things both their parents respect, even enthusiasm as mistaken as this is, I swallow down my remarks about "Long past bedtime," and William drives off to Piccadilly to join the circus and circle round and round in the revolving traffic, the lights pouring changing colours over our faces as we pass.

At the back of the car the children kneel on the seat, as children do when they are excited. They crouch at the windows, one at each side, gazing out unblinking at the astonishing world which spins around them. Peter is silent with delight, John exclaims in excitement at each new wonder. No pleasure could be simpler nor easier to come by. But alas, it will not last. It will wear off as quickly, I imagine, as the pleasure is already wearing off my household shopping in the High Street, as the fluffy halo withers from mimosa flowers in a single day, leaving small dull pellets. It is only that night for the children till now has meant simply sleep; that they lived in a world where fields and houses when the sun went down were drowned in darkness as profound and lonely as the bottom of the sea. How could they ever have guessed that this entrancing pageant went on at the end of the village road which led to London?

"And I like the clumps of red buses," said Peter, "and all the bunches of people." Does he see the buses tall like trees, I wonder, and the people crowded together like bundles of rhubarb?

"But I don't like London ladies," said John decidedly one day at tea-time, coming in from school. "I don't like their clickety high heels on the pavement," he said, considering them critically against his six-year background of flat-heeled farmers' wives and the comfortable keepers of village shops.

"No," agreed Peter, a year older but with tastes just as rustic. "But what I hate most of all is when they have ear-rings that go right through their ears. I think it's horrid," and he screwed up his sensitive face in disgust. "It makes me not like any ear-rings at all."

"Yes, I know," said John in comforting agreement, two normal men already most happily united in their dislike of fashion. "And I don't like their little thin waists," he went on. "There isn't enough room for everything to go up and down inside." John considered their thinness with scorn. "And I'm sure they can't swim. Not at all. They'd sink to the bottom."

For John has a theory he has worked out for himself: that to swim you must be fat—the fatter the better—and that if you could be quite mountainously fat you would be the best swimmer in the whole world.

"Why do you think so?" I asked him once. "Oh, everyone knows that," he answered with contemptuous conviction. "Look at whales."

No doubt in time they will change their opinions about high heels and the smallness of waists, but just now London ladies are not in the least what they admire or approve of.

"And they *will* wear evening dresses," Peter goes on with his list of complaints. "We see them in shop windows when we're going on the bus. And I don't like it." (He is very pompous.) "It makes them look like dolls."

"Besides," John joins in indignantly, "they wear their dresses even in the day-time and even when they're not going to parties."

I can see that anything more frivolous than corduroy trousers must seem to these country children like evening dress, and I wonder if John's next attack is meant for me, since I no longer wear the trousers and jerseys he is used to, but get up every day in the clothes he thought were only for parties.

"It upsets their husbands," John is indignant, "because they can't tell if their wives are staying in or going out."

They seem to get most extraordinary impressions of the town from their daily bus-rides to school, but what they do whole-heartedly like in London is the new school itself. They are delighted to progress from their country kindergarten of boys and girls together, to this new man's world of cricket and football and prefects, and a real cane for the first time hanging over the fire-place in the headmaster's study as an awful warning. They are particularly proud of the cane. They see it as a symbol that they have left childish things behind them in their nursery classes, that they are half-way at least to manhood, and this school is the real right thing.

As for the discipline, that they accept cheerfully as a matter of course, and have already arranged their private lives to their own satisfaction within the framework of school rules. For I am a strict old-fashioned parent, and they are quite used to obeying the accepted laws. The cane they recognize perfectly well for what it is: a reasonable token of adult authority, like my token slapping when they were babies. They will not be caned, they know quite well, unless they deserve it, and that they consider is fair: unpleasant but not alarming.

What they found much more startling than the school rules, is the rules of cricket.

"Did you know that school cricket's quite different to ours?" asked Peter in astonishment after his first games afternoon. "In school cricket they've lots and *lots* of rules." For their cricket till now has been a simple game of bat and ball for two people, played against a tree-trunk for wicket and the orchard for cricket-pitch. It was a very impromptu game with only four fixed rules of any importance, and these were all for the batter. If he missed the ball he must fetch it and throw it back to the bowler. If he hit the ball into the long grass he must help to find it. If he hit it into the stream he must go and get it out himself. If he hit it into the cow-yard he was out.

"But did you know," asked Peter in the high up and down voice of complete astonishment, "in school cricket you don't just have *one* wicket, you have *two?*" He waits for me to be as incredulous as he clearly is. "And you have *two* boys and *two* bats! And it's a rule that they mustn't both be at the same end together. And when they hit the ball they don't have to watch and see where it's going in the grass like we do. They have lots and *lots* of people to find it for them, not just the one that throws it, and that's called fielding." He stops and looks at me wide-eyed, giving me time to recover from my amazement, for there is more to come. "And it's a rule that when you're fielding you *must* keep running about. You mustn't stop and pick flowers—not even when there's nothing happening. And you mustn't go and watch the trains either (only we can't help looking) and most of all you *mustn't* have fights with your friends. That makes them crosser than anything."

Peter pauses to consider these quite unexpected restrictions of the game, and goes on in a lower voice, as if in parenthesis, "But that's really a Football Rule—that you mustn't have fights at *all*, except where the ball is, and then it doesn't matter because in football you're *meant* to."

But what does astonish me, what I really would like to know, is not so much the rules themselves, which I had after all suspected, but who can have explained them to an audience so unexpectedly ignorant. Did the games master solemnly forbid, I wonder, the watching of trains and the picking of daisies? Did two small boys with two large bats stand side by side at the same wicket before he separated them? But I daresay it was only Peter who was so wonderfully innocent, and he is no help when I ask him who told him the proper behaviour.

"Oh, *every*one knows about cricket," he says airily. "*Any*one will tell you the rules."

So I shall find out no more about cricket, and must content myself with noticing that he has already made friends at school to fight with. For it is their friends that small boys fight with, not their enemies. Enemies are an unpleasantness best avoided unless there is no other way but battle, and the game of rough-and-tumble which they call fighting needs friends for partners, not enemies. It is a kind of hearty embrace which they only engage in with companions they find sympathetic, rolling about together on the floor, sitting on top of each other, scuffling and yelling and thumping and tickling, till they both roll apart at last, too exhausted and breathless with laughter to go on any longer.

At this age it is the most satisfactory of games both for children and parents, for although there are few things more tiresome than small boys rolling on the floor like puppies round our feet when we are busy, yet it is a sure sign of fair weather, we know they feel at home and confident.

For John there was no hesitation. He confronts his life with frank enjoyment, finding his own pleasures, and he came home in the first week at school with cheerful tales of his encounters.

"I had a *lovely* fight with a boy to-day. *He* put his head down and charged at me, and *I* whirled my arms round and went wind-milling into him, and we hit each other so hard we both fell over," and so on and so on.

But Peter would listen and say nothing. He is a serious creature not much given to romping, and he takes much longer than John to settle down. But even Peter I notice, now talks of fights with his friends, he begins to feel at his ease. For already they both grow confident in their new life, begin to find their way about by themselves in this different existence where everything is changed from what they knew before—the house they live in, the school where they spend their day, the outside world they pass through travelling backwards and forwards. Nothing here survives of all their old familiar universe except the furniture and me. And even the furniture is different, oddly arranged in new strange rooms so that it no longer seems familiar. No wonder I have had to hold their hands till now so firmly and so patiently.

Years ago I once watched a monkey which had been taught to do tricks so that the psychologists could test its intelligence. Dif-ficult tricks they had to be clearly, almost too difficult even for a monkey, so that the investigators could find the utmost limit of its mental powers. It was a nice monkey, clever and gentle and affectionate, and because it was very eager to please, it learned to do quite complicated tasks, tasks almost beyond the skill of any animal, even an animal as intelligent as this one.

Whatever it was asked to do in the tests, it did at once, very quickly and nervously with worried movements, restless and fidgeting, driven by the never-ending anxiety of being asked to do always just a little more than it could understand. And in its eyes, looking constantly into our faces to see if we were pleased, was the profound trouble of a half-intelligent creature bewildered on the verge of understanding.

It has haunted me ever since. And often in these last months with the children I have been reminded of the monkey, seeing in their faces, in Peter's especially, the same anxious bewilderment, the same eagerness to do what was expected without being able to understand.

But already they are losing their nervous hurry, are growing gay and careless again as they were before. Although they are still half strangers in the town, and their ordinary day is still no doubt alarmingly full of surprises, yet in the flux which still surrounds them there are islands now of solid ground where they feel they can plant their feet firmly, and keep their balance without my help while they interpret to their own satisfaction this exciting new world they now inhabit.

I too am bewildered by London; not by the traffic as the children are, but by the consciousness of other people so close all around me. For living in a town we live as animals in a herd, companionably. We grow used to the near presence of our fellow-creatures all about us. Yet although we live so close to each other, within sight and sound of our neighbours, we are not disturbed by their nearness. We concentrate on our own life, and the other lives all about us are only the urban background of our day, as the life of the farm was our background in the country. Without conscious selection we ignore in a community the sounds and movements which do not concern us, we hear only the voices which are speaking to us in particular. But living so long without neighbours I am no longer a community animal. In my private country world, if a fellow-creature appeared then he did concern me. When he spoke he was speaking to me and no one else. If there were sounds and movements around me, then I must find out what they were—the sheep got through the garden hedge perhaps and eating the daffodils, or one of the children out of bed in the night.

And it is not only out-of-doors in a town that I hear too much. Even in the quiet house my senses of a solitary animal are disturbed all day by the constant small sounds of human beings on every side. I listen. Moving quietly about the house as people move who live in quiet places, as animals do, I stop still a hundred times a day to listen—to the slight vague knocks and thumps of people moving in the houses on each side of us, to the distant voices of the workmen in the mews, the caretaker in the basement clattering the tea-cups in the sink, the faint hum of the lift next door, to a far-off telephone bell, and now and again the alarm of louder noises from the street outside.

I must stop and listen to every slight disturbance before I realize it is nothing to do with me. Soon, I know, the unfamiliar noises will blur together to an unheard background texture of companionable living. Soon I shall hear only the sounds which concern me in this general web. My unconscious ears will grow selective, as our ears are in sleep, rousing us only to attend to the sounds which matter for us in particular; so that we wake at once for the faintest cry of our children, but sleep like the deaf through the hooting of owls and the roar of the wind in the trees.

But not yet. I am not yet conditioned. I am still aware and listen to each separate sound, like an animal put suddenly in a zoo, uneasily conscious of unfamiliar neighbours. And living so long alone in the country with the children who do not count, I had developed the vague speechless senses we share with the animals. I knew if someone had been to the house while I was away, could tell if a stranger had walked down a path unseen ahead of me, and if someone had turned in at the far field gate I knew they were coming, as animals know, before they were within sight or hearing. As Lapps, they say, living alone in their forests, know when strangers are approaching, though still a day's journey away. So that set down suddenly in this thronging centre of a city, I am as bewildered by the many presences as someone with acute hearing must be confused by a constant hubbub of sound. I still know, before they knock, when someone is on the doorstep; I still go to pick up the telephone before it rings. But it is a troubled sense now, like trying to listen to faint sounds through a distracting noise, and I shall be glad to lose it.

Nor is it only the life all about me which distracts my consciousness with unwanted perceptions. Like a long-learned habit which still persists though we need it no longer, my old life still interrupts the new. I have not yet left the country properly behind me; and as when people we have grown used to go away from us, and we find ourselves wondering from hour to hour of the day where they are now and what they are doing, so I wonder suddenly, for no reason at all, what is happening in the places I am used to. Will the light be shining on the hills perhaps? Or is it raining? Is the orchard in blossom? Will the cowman now be calling up the cows to come lurching heavily in through the buttercups to the milking shed?

A dozen times a day I look out through the window to study the weather, as I have looked out for years each morning before I planned our day. For in the country the weather is the most important thing that happens. We must arrange our lives to suit it as we need not do in a town. Here the weather is no more than a pleasure or an inconvenience, and in time no doubt I shall lose this habit of looking so often at the sky beyond the window, even though now I am still conscious of the climate in the open which has governed my life for so long; as sea-anemones, land-locked in inland aquariums, still open and close to the remembered rhythm of the distant tides.

It is not that I languish for the open air—I am thoroughly glad to be free of the weather: not that I want to be back with the cows and the orchard and the light on the hills. Not in the least. I have come back to London and here I want to stay. The anonymous society of my fellow-creatures all around me is friendly and comfortable after the alien cows. I am delighted to hear human voices instead of hens outside the window, to open the door on to a street full of people like myself.

But I do not belong here yet. I am not at my ease. And one of the troubles of London—though I can see that quite quickly it will not be a trouble at all but a fascination—is the difficulty at first that as a setting for our lives a great city is so much more vast than we can ever encompass. We cannot grasp what is going on all around us, cannot compose the multitudinous life of this metropolis into a comprehensible whole, so that we feel at home with the background we live against.

In the country it is different. We can easily understand the life of a village. We know, or can very well guess, just what is going on in the streets and shops and houses, on the farms and in the work-yards. The business of the country banks and old-fashioned offices and local estate agents is business we can understand because it is related to our own lives more or less closely. We know who lives in all the houses, and what goes on behind all the windows in the High Street. The people we pass are familiar, they are busy with their accustomed affairs; and if we meet an occasional stranger, we generally know as well as he does himself exactly where he is going—to the auction sale at the farm on the hill, or to look at the cottage with the yew-tree at the gate, which is empty now since the station-master died.

I suppose this familiarity is why young people are restless in a village, are drawn away to the cities by the strangeness and excitement and opportunity of the unknown. For the life of London is so complex and various that to any one person most of it must always be unknown. There are so many different worlds in the same city: the world of shops and fashion, Parliament and all the affairs of government, the Port of London with its docks and the ships from the open seas, the commercial City with telephone lines circling the world, New York from one desk, Hong Kong from another. There is the river with its different watery life governed by the up-and-down wash of the tides, Fleet Street and the world of newspapers, the museums like telescopes looking into the wide landscape of past history, the art galleries, the University, the markets, hotels, theatres, Law Courts—a bewildering complexity of different worlds, each of them elaborate and self-contained, all superimposed on each other to make the supreme complexity which is London. Even the familiar pavements stream with strangers, busy people preoccupied with affairs we cannot even guess at. In every direction buses roll off to unimaginable destinations. The life of the city is layer upon layer of strangeness.

It is alarming at first to feel ourselves surrounded on every side by activities we cannot understand. For by things which are strange we are easily frightened: the unknown turns quickly sinister when it is darkened by the faintest shadow. And in London at first there is altogether too much that is unknown. In time no doubt we grow used to the unencompassed. Confident within our own familiar life, we feel ourselves safely at home in our own small world, and the rest of London no more than a pageant beyond our windows. We shall not be troubled by the complex background of unknown activity, but come to value it as a mysterious depth behind the familiar surface of our daily living, only conscious of it dimly as the stimulation of life in a city. We shall only now and then be vividly aware of the unseen worlds revolving all around us—when we wait perhaps while policemen hold up the traffic for some official car to slide past to Westminster, or hear at night, when the wind blows from the south, the far-off mournful hooting of the boats we had forgotten, down on the river, waiting for the tide to turn.

The very size of London is alarming, the actual physical extent of bricks and mortar, for no-one can be familiar with a city of ten million people. There are alien miles of undiscovered territory for every small district we know. Great stretches of strangeness surround us on every side, it will always be strange, glimpsed now and then from the tops of hills and high buildings and filling us with dismay. Shall we ever find our way, we wonder despairingly, in this grey chaos of building which stretches to the horizon in every direction. It is not only the people and their lives which we cannot encompass, but the city itself.

And because I am not yet a city dweller but still a cousin come in from the country, I am grateful for the things which remind me of my familiar country background. The trees in the squares are not for me simply the green decoration of the city which their planters intended; they are a happy reassurance that if they can live serenely in this bewildering new environment, then so can I. I look up at the narrow sky over the houses, the wider sky over the parks, and see with relief that the sailing clouds are the same familiar shapes that I know, that even above London the sky is still countrified, with birds flying over. At night the moon, which seems in some places a remote and mysterious presence, is here a visiting friend. And so that we shall recognize our house in its row of similar houses, I have planted trees in tubs on the steps, one each side of the doorway where I stand in green like a garden to hunt for the latch-key I am not yet used to carrying.

Yet why do I make so much fuss, I wonder, about coming back to London? For I have lived here before, lived and worked happily for years and never wanted to go away. But that was long ago, and every so often—is it every seven years they say? —we outgrow our old selves and turn into new people with all our world to learn over again. Or perhaps it is that living so close to the children all these years, sharing their moods and reactions, I feel London as they feel it, and try to find reasons for the vague misgivings and inexplicable alarms which I catch from them in sympathy.

But already after these first few months we are all of us over the first violent transplanting of our animal senses from country calm to city centre. In the house the children are already at home, settled in their own bedrooms as snug and familiar as animals in their burrows. Already they move about without looking, as we move in places we know well, sure of our way even in the dark. In my household drawers and cupboards they already know far better than I do where things are, where to find the tools they want, the nails and scissors and pieces of string, all the equipment so mysteriously necessary in the private lives of boys. They have transplanted more quickly than I have, being more malleable.

At school too they are now completely at their ease. They have accepted the rules, learned the hierarchies, and found which masters can be trifled with and which not. Already they have made up their minds about which boys are friends and which enemies, have discovered all the taboos and privileges of the world of school, which after all was arranged for boys like themselves, and is therefore perfectly comprehensible if they consider it with detachment.

They are full of enthusiasm for what they consider their first real lessons, sitting in rows at desks now, with men to teach them instead of women. They are scornful of the bottom class which cannot read or write, and they come home delighted with their first homework in the new leather satchels they carry so proudly after the linen shoe-bags of their kindergarten days.

"For my prep to-night I've got to draw a picture out of the Bible," John announces importantly, settling down with his paper and crayons at the kitchen table. For the room we use as a kitchen was once a library, a long pleasant room with an arched ceiling and a triple window looking out into a yard of white-washed walls, where I have planted laurels and pots of geraniums and a vine to grow up the house and frame the window. And because it was a library so long before we came, the room still keeps a faintly bookish air despite the sink and the gas-stove and the pots and pans in the cupboards. And in the evening, when once the tea-things are cleared away, the long kitchen table changes its character and becomes once more a table in a library. It is why no doubt, the kitchen seems the natural place for the children's homework, though I *must*, Peter tells me, *must*, now they go to a proper boys' school, remember to call it their Prep.

So to-night we sit, me at the end of the table, Peter and John each side, all with our books, for I too find that I sit and read in this kitchen-library with vine leaves round the window. We settle down and no-one talks.

John is half-lying, sprawled across the table, his nose no more than an inch from his picture, as children always sprawl, writing or reading. But now he sits up, considers his drawing critically and turns it upside down. He looks up at me and smiles without speaking. And I think how suddenly older he has become, outgrowing his first childhood. For young children seldom smile at us like that, in simple goodwill from one person to another. Young children smile (or more often laugh) because they are excited or happy, and if they smile at us it is only because we are mixed up with their pleasure. It is not at us as a person in our own right that they smile, but only in our relationship to them. I think for small children we scarcely exist as individuals apart from themselves. They do not look up at us as John does now, considering me quietly, smiling with peaceful affection as we smile at our friends.

He heaves an enormous sigh, turns his picture the right way up again and licks his pencil energetically. "I've nearly finished," he says. "Then I'll show you."

We settle down again and I go back to my book. Peter has left us. He got up quietly some time ago and went off upstairs without a word, busy with his own concerns. There is silence in the kitchen until John has finished his homework, is satisfied at last with his Bible picture and brings it to me for an opinion.

"Do you like it?" he asks, leaning against me and looking at it proudly over my shoulder, waiting for me to admire.

THE LAST SUPPER it states confidently at the top, and certainly I can see that the scene is a group of people at a table, so I suppose the general conception will do. But about the details I feel more doubtful. Across the top of the picture at the far side of the table is a row of figures, and between all the figures are chairs. The chairs are drawn side-view and the figures are standing up. There is no attempt to mould the figures to the chairs, but all the same I think they are meant to be sitting down for supper. I can see that there are technical difficulties about drawing people, especially seated people, and that is probably why the men are all turned sideways as well as the chairs, like the men in the Bayeux Tapestry. So I mentally turn the whole row round to face me, turn their chairs round behind them and sit them all down. I only hope that is what John intended.

What I do know for certain is that they are meant to be men not women, for John's women are always the same, dressed in a short full skirt like a half-opened umbrella, and their heads encircled by a huge scribbled cloud of curly hair. Since these figures have neither skirts nor hair then I know they must be men. Yet though they are bald and bare-legged, several of the men have enormous walrus moustaches, and most of them have hats. (But should they really be wearing their hats at table, even if I am wrong about the chairs and they are not meant to be sitting down?) Jesus—it is his only garment—wears a kind of trilby, and floating serenely some way above it a carefully-drawn halo. It makes him look very tall, but not for me very convincing.

I try to free my mind of preconceived ideas, as they say we should when looking at works of art. I try to get rid of my prejudices about what sacred figures should look like. But no. I can't, I simply *can't* feel happy about the hat. Not the hat *and* the halo both together. One or other—yes. But both at once I simply cannot manage. However hard I try to see with an innocent eye, they still look odd to me as a combination.

As for what the party would have for supper with their hats on, that I had never really thought about. Bread, I supposed, and wine, and perhaps something vaguely symbolic like fruit or fish. But John has thought about the supper with great concentra-

tion: it has clearly been for him the main point of the picture.
For every inch of the enormous table is covered with dishes
which are not in the least vague or symbolic but very exact. I
suppose it is why his Bible picture has taken so long to finish, for
certainly the figures are no more than the perfunctory tokens of
men which he dashes off in a few minutes' scribbling. But the
supper itself is in an altogether different style, realistic enough to
recognize each separate dish. There are plates of chocolate biscuits, of cream buns and meringues, there are jellies rising up
from the table in intricate and lovingly-observed turrets and
pyramids, and there is a bowl of what I think is meant to be fruit
salad, since it is John's favourite dish. And all these delicacies are
drawn in such detail that they have come out far larger than the
figures round the table. The chocolate biscuits are as big as suitcases, the bowl of fruit salad would do for a bath, and as for the
jellies—they are turretted castles huge enough for the entire
supper-party to sit inside if they wanted.

But the focus of the picture, the centre-piece of the table set
exactly in front of Jesus, is an enormous iced cake. It is raised a
little on a ceremonial dish, it is beautifully decorated, and it is
crowned—not with birthday candles, since that would clearly
introduce a quite unsuitably frivolous note, and since this is not
in any case a *birthday* supper—it is crowned triumphantly with
a cross.

"Do you think it's good?" John understandably is not quite
convinced and needs reassurance. "I'm not very good at drawing
people. That's why they have to be sideways. And you see that
thing coming out of the ceiling that looks like a tongue? Well,
that's the Holy Ghost. Do you think that people will know that
it is?"

Certainly *I* did not know, but perhaps the "people" John
means are more used than I am to Bible pictures drawn by six-
year-olds.

"I think it's a very good picture," I assure him, avoiding such point-blank enquiries. "Only you know it isn't really polite for men to wear their hats at table." (Since I cannot teach him religion, I may as well take the chance to teach him manners.) But John brushes aside such finicking objections.

"I don't suppose anyone minded in those days," he airily assures me. "I don't suppose they *knew* about manners in the old days."

I can see that as creative artists nothing makes us more self-confident than criticism of inessentials, and I cannot help wondering whether the subject was not in any case set chiefly for the amusement of the setter. But now with his homework finished and approved, John is drawing to please himself, drawing in a fiddling old-fashioned style, would-be accurate pictures of aeroplanes and space-ships and racing motor-cars racing up hills as steep as roof-tops. For he has already outgrown the uninhibited modern-art style which seems to be natural to all small children, and which we adults nowadays so whole-heartedly admire. Once his Christmas trees were great velvety presences blotting out a purple sky, deep green backgrounds splodged and daubed with every vividest colour for decoration. But now they are thin and spiky, trying to look like fir-trees, and the hanging decorations are drawn each in most careful undecorative detail. But all true artists must paint to please themselves, and John now likes to see the spokes in wheels and the exact construction of a propellor.

"What does maroon mean?" he suddenly asks, looking up from his drawing. It is a question from nowhere, as children's questions so often are for adults, since our minds travel over such different kinds of country.

"It's a colour," I tell him, "a dark browny-red."

John is puzzled but polite.

"I really don't think it can be. It's something nasty you do to people on desert islands. You *maroon* them. In the picture they sit on the sand and there's a dead skull at the side of them and they don't look happy. Only I don't know why they call it a *desert* island," he goes on scornfully, "when it's grown all over with banana trees and coconut trees and all things to eat."

Well neither do I. It is one of the conventions I suppose, like all princesses having yellow hair, and Chinese tigers being friendly.

But our discussion is interrupted by the insistent patter of someone learning to use a typewriter in the next room, and John rushes off to watch his father, scattering crayons as he goes.

Because there are so many times when his part-time secretary is not about when he wants her, William has bought an old type-writer and is teaching himself to type. "William's Little Buttons," the children call it, and watch him intently, quite clearly envious of this most superior toy which grown-ups keep for their own amusement. No doubt they too hope to have a turn in time, if they are patient and do not ask too soon. But they know they must wait, understanding very well from their own experience that we never want anyone else to touch our newest treasures.

William likes to do things in a hurry, and has no patience at all with books on Teach Yourself Typing and quick brown foxes jumping about. He simply sits in front of his Buttons and types out with one or two fingers whatever comes into his head. Poetry it mostly is, nursery rhymes and scraps of doggerel, odd snatches of Marvell and bits from Keats's Odes. But he never can remember more than a line or so at a time, and to-night it is a pastiche of Shakespeare's Sonnets, single first lines mostly, since that is what we all remember, so that what comes mangled out of the type-writer is not an anthology of poems but a kaleidoscope of poetical snippets. And they are very mangled indeed—all joined together without warning or punctuation or capital letters, with wrong spelling, wrong spacing, words run together or chopped off short in the middle, run off the end of the line—all the curiously undignified mistakes of beginners' first typing. No one could help but think of Shaw's monkeys.

The First Three Years Transplanted

Yet still the poetry of the Sonnets blazes through as I read the first lines over William's shoulder.

> *"Farewell! thou art too dear for my possessing,"*
> *"Shall I compare thee to a summer's day?"*
> *"When in disgrace with fortune and men's eyes"*

The Sonnets seem always the very quintessence of poetry, powerful, profound, incorruptible, surviving all hazards.

In the gap between William's shoulder and the children's crowding heads, I watch fascinated as two consecutive lines jerk slowly out without mistakes.

> *"When to the sessions of sweet silent thought*
> *"I summon up remembrance of things past,"*

William is not limited to poetry however, but has a fine catholic range of taste which includes a particular liking for *In Memoriams* in original verse, and accounts of country weddings in local newspapers. He is copying one now from the paper we brought back from the country at the week-end, typing straight on without a break at the end of his sonnet medley. "The bride was attired in a gown of rose-pink satin with a fichu of pale blue net."

"What's a fichu?" William asks, with no interruption of his typing. "Why do they always wear a fichu?"

I suspect that the reporter has no more idea than William of what a fichu really is but has simply picked up the word as a suitable word for weddings. "She wore a wreath of orange-blossom and forget-me-nots." But what a pity he cannot copy the photograph as well; the bridegroom awkward—shamefaced almost—for this is a woman's game (we can almost hear him muttering rebelliously) this posing in front of cameras. Much happier he'd be (and he looks very manly and strong) tossing bales of hay, or slamming in the gears of tractors, than standing about like this, hot in his best blue suit with his collar too tight, feeling a fool.

But the bride is delighted to have her rose-pink satin recorded. She smiles with pleasure and pure good-nature, her face as shiny as her satin. Plump and pleased, she will make the most comfortable of mothers.

"As the happy couple walked down the aisle the wedding bells rang out a joyous peal." What the children make of all this I have no idea, nor even whether they can read it; for they make no comment, but only watch fascinated in silent dismay as William goes typing off the edge of the paper without noticing, far too occupied with finding the right buttons to tap.

But it is late for the children to be up, they must go to bed now, I tell them, and at once they break out in a clamour of protest. Most nights they merely grumble and go, but to-night they argue, feeling perhaps that William will support them as a powerful ally against me. For they have lived with William for so short a time yet that he is still an unknown quantity in their world. There is a great deal still to find out about this stranger in their lives, and who knows? perhaps he will be on their side, not mine, in this business of bedtime. Certainly it is worth trying, and there follows one of our rare but periodic arguments about what time they should go to bed.

They are not defiant, for they know very well that if they defy me I shall insist on winning at once, they will both be bundled off upstairs in a trice and no more nonsense. The argument is not even about going to bed to-night in particular, but concerns that fundamental principle in children's lives: what time in general they should be expected to go to bed. They are law-abiding citizens, but they like to make the laws to suit themselves. I can quite see, it is the perfect arrangement.

"No-one at school goes to bed as early as we do. *No-one.*" John complains in an injured voice, talking half to me and half to William, who does not listen.

. 28 .

The First Three Years Transplanted

"My best friend never goes to bed till ten o'clock." John watches me, waiting for me to exclaim in horror. But I say nothing and he makes a defiant gesture to impress me.

"Sometimes he doesn't go to bed till *eleven*."

I recognize this very well for what it is—the usual boasting of small boys, who for some reason love always to brag about how late they go to bed, as if staying up late made them heroes of some mysterious adventure of darkness and night. But I know about these mythical friends who stay up till midnight (for it will certainly be midnight in John's next pronouncement). I have met their mothers. "Does your boy really stay up till all hours?" I have asked them.

"No. Certainly not." The answer is always the same. "I bundle him off to bed just as soon as I possibly can."

But to-night's argument about bedtime is still going on.

"What we ought to do," says Peter judicially, in the high surprised voice of someone discovering an unexpected truth. "What we *ought* to do . . ." and he produces again, as they have already produced before in the same discussion on other occasions, the reasonable-sounding argument that I suppose all children must have used to all parents ever since bedtimes were insisted on—that children should go to bed at the hour of their ages: seven o'clock at seven years old, eight o'clock at eight.

Since Peter will soon be eight, and since they naturally reckon both by the higher age, they could stay up now, they hopefully suggest, till nearly eight o'clock. But it is an argument which becomes quite quickly impracticable, and is clearly impossible somewhere in the late teens, however one reckons. For even John, most confirmed of stayers-up, is dismayed by the thought that he would never see bed again after his twenty-fourth birthday.

"Well, can't we go *half* an hour later now we're nearly a whole year older?"

They realize this is a sensible proposal and make it in quiet sensible voices, waiting for an answer, not flinging it out in bravado as they did with their boasting of midnight.

I look at them both and consider my tactics, for our relations with children on the subject of bedtime are not at all simple. There is no question of this being merely a friendly exchange: it is diplomacy of the highest order, as we all well know. I may be determined, but so are they, and very wily. They know a score of ways for slowing up bedtime without any actual defiance—sudden hunger, or teeth not cleaned, or things to get ready for morning. And I am not prepared to argue with them every night; we must agree about times and they must go off with no more ado when I tell them.

Ever since we came to London they have been going to bed later and later, for we arrived with our country ways of bed with the sun and up with the lark, and we have changed, like changing to winter time after summer, rearranged our habits to city fashions of turning night to day and sleeping half the morning. For me it gives the ordinary working-day a wonderfully luxurious sense of lying abed and leisure, of staying up quite frivolously late every night of the week.

But the children, once indoors, have no further consciousness of clocks. They have no idea what time they really go to bed, except that it is always, if they can manage it, a little later than authority intended. So now I can concede their extra half hour, solemnly, diplomatically, exacting in return enthusiastic promises that they will—they really *will*—*always* from now on wash themselves properly clean, and brush their teeth without telling.

I have no qualms at all about cheating on my side, for I know very well, and so do they, that after the first few days of improvement they will be just as dirty when I come to inspect them in the bath at night, and their teeth will be just as forgotten. But they will have won by then their extra half hour, a treasured victory and almost impossible to reverse.

Though why John should mind going to bed I can never see,

for he settles down with a smile of beatific comfort, and falls asleep the moment he pulls the blankets up to his chin. John sleeps as enthusiastically as he wakes. It is Peter who is uneasy at night, who lies tossing for hours after I have said Good night, fidgeting and over-tired, too restless to lie still and sleep after the bewildering excitement of his London day. So that Peter and I have come to an unspoken agreement together: that if he is still awake and hears the chimes of the nine-o'clock news, he may come downstairs quietly without waking John, and sit beside me till he feels better.

So now on his bad nights, before the nine-o'clock chimes are over, the sitting-room door opens a few apologetic inches and Peter's head comes diffidently round to make sure that I am alone. Reassured, he opens the door a very little further and edges in with a rueful smile, walks round the room like a cat behind the chairs and tables to reach where I am sitting, and settles down with a long sigh of relief.

Peter is a dignified creature and considers that this is quite unsuitably childish behaviour in a person of his advanced age. He only comes because he must come, or else lie awake endlessly tossing. But because he is intolerant in matters which concern his own dignity, there is an understanding between us that I shall never give any sign that I have noticed his arrival except to make room for him beside me, and that I must never speak except to rouse him when I feel him growing too drowsy to walk up to bed again. For these visits downstairs are for Peter a charm beyond the power of poppies, a charm which stills his fidgeting as simply and completely as unhooking the wires of a puppet. Heavy, happy, boneless, he goes back straight to sleep.

There was an evening when John managed for once not to fall asleep the instant he settled in bed, and came downstairs instead of Peter. He must somehow have suspected that he was missing some secret evening privilege granted only to those a year older, that Peter was admitted to some mysterious social occasion that he knew nothing of, but now at last would find out for himself.

One the last stroke of nine he appeared in the doorway and stood smiling expectantly. He had put on the coat of his pyjamas I noticed, had dressed up for his visit; for he thinks it more manly to sleep in the trousers alone: only softies, he says, wear pyjama jackets.

"Do come in," I invite him, turning off the wireless. "Come in and sit down."

He walks confidently across the room and settles himself in William's chair at the opposite side of the fireplace. He folds his arms and crosses his legs in an adult conversational way, though with one knee over the other his feet no longer reach the hearth-rug.

JOHN: Where's William?

ME: He's at a hospital committee.

JOHN: What's a committee?

ME: It's when a lot of doctors sit round a table and discuss things—like how to make the hospital better.

There is a pause while John digests this promising new information.

"Yes, I see. Sometimes they don't like the nurses and sack them. And sometimes the nurses don't like the hospital and sack it."

Sack is a new word recently learned, and I think it is only so that he can make use of it that John starts off his committee-meeting so ruthlessly, for he is not naturally quarrelsome. He goes on more cheerfully:

"Then they think they'd like ice-cream for lunch every day. So they say to have it and not have any meat." John considers this diet with satisfaction, then suddenly realizes that his power is absolute. "And ice-cream for breakfast too—just whenever we wanted. And they say to get more comics for the children—lots and lots of comics—all the comics there are in the world."

A committee, John clearly sees, is the ideal way of setting about things. I watch him across the hearthrug, sitting up straight in his chair with concentration, vividly awake, not looking in the least like bed. He considers his own stay in hospital and wonders what other improvements he can suggest.

But he thoroughly enjoyed himself. There was nothing really he could complain of except—Oh yes, there was the cricket.

"They could say that it was a rule that wickets must be painted on the door of the children's ward so that we could all play cricket in the corridor whenever we wanted."

(The ward had never been so cheerful, the nurses said, as the week John was there. Nor so noisy, they said, sighing even to remember.)

"But they wouldn't let you play cricket," I remind him. "You made too much noise."

"No," John agrees, "but they could have a committee and say the noise didn't matter. And *we* could have a committee too," John always pursues his ideas with energy. "We could all have one here about how to make the house better."

There is another pause while he considers this new development. I watch his face and try to guess what he will suggest. Something about bedtime, I imagine, and I am right.

"Well. Me and Peter would like to go to bed an *hour* later, not just *half* an hour. And we'd like to have pocket-money every day, not just every week. Because just every week isn't enough you know, because in London the shops are there every day."

This seems to John so perfectly reasonable that he does not bother to notice my reactions. But the next request is not so straightforward and he watches my face carefully as he speaks.

"When you're cross I'd like *never* to be scolded but always be punished instead."

This is a *cri de coeur* I never expected, and John goes on feelingly, "I *hate* being scolded—it makes me feel so sad. And I don't a bit mind being punished."

Well, I mind both, since I like to be friends, but of the two I prefer the scolding. It seems more natural and less vindictive to

fly out at them while I am still annoyed than to withhold deliberately, in calculated cold blood, some long-looked-for pleasure. I
daresay it is why I am so clearly inefficient at the punishing.

But John is still talking. He has a strong innate feeling for the
social occasions and he seems to feel that as my visitor to-night it
is for him to find subjects of conversation.

JOHN: I miss Granny, don't you?
ME: Yes, I do.
JOHN: I wish she was with us here.
ME: Yes, so do I.
JOHN: I wonder what she's doing now.
ME: I expect she's fast asleep in bed.

I realize too late that this is a most ungracious way to speak to
an evening visitor, even though he may have come to call on me
uninvited. There is no excuse. But if John notices the hint to go
he decides to ignore it. He merely talks of something else in a
bland untroubled way which may be deliberate or may be unconscious, for already with John there is no way of knowing
how many levels of consciousness he can move on at once. I think
most children are far more subtle than we like to believe.

John settles down more comfortably in a corner of his large
chair. In the lamplight his hair shines with the same soft gloss as
the children's hair in Velasquez's portraits, and his eyelashes are
so long and thick that they make a shadowed fringe on his smooth
pink cheeks.

"I had a funny dream last night," he begins again. But this time
I shall certainly not encourage him, for of all the possible things
to talk about, nothing is as unprofitably boring as other people's
dreams. It is not only that the dreams are of no interest to us, but
the dreamers themselves are always so tiresomely proud of them,
as if they had done something quite wonderfully clever and unu-
sual in dreaming as we all do.

But John is only making conversation and his dream is merci-
fully short.

The First Three Years Transplanted

"I dreamed it was raining and an elephant nudged me."

Certainly it is one of the more interesting dreams, for what kind of terms does one have to be on with an elephant before it starts nudging? Nudging to me means a particular kind of knowing intimacy—like a wink. But with an *elephant?* And *how* does it nudge? Were they sitting side by side perhaps, on a bench in the rain?

But I say nothing to John, for if we once encourage people to talk about their dreams there is never any stopping them. I once knew someone who wrote down his dreams as soon as he woke in the morning. He kept pencil and paper always by his bed on purpose, and whenever I met him and remembered, my spirits sank to gloom.

But John is not a boring dreamer and is already talking of something quite different.

"You know those big boards they have all along the streets with pictures on?"

ME: Yes. They're called posters. They're advertisements.

JOHN: And you know how it always says *that* thing's best— whatever it is?

ME: Yes. Advertisements always do.

JOHN: Well, who decides what to say?

ME: The people who sell the things.

(I can see very well where we are going, but I am driven along without a chance to escape, like the unsuspecting young men Socrates was so fond of driving into absurd conclusions.)

JOHN: Well, isn't it boasting?

(He pauses, not because he wants an answer, but pauses in triumph, as I daresay Socrates did too.)

JOHN: And isn't it rude to boast? And anyway how do you know it's true if they only say it is themselves?

This unanswerable logic is propounded with the utmost scorn and conviction, and ever since he has never mentioned advertisements except as Those Boasters. "Those Boasters," he says in

contempt, glaring disdainfully at the huge posters for soap pow-
ders he passes in the bus. And he comes home with cynical questions. "To-day I saw on one of Those Boasters it says that in an
aeroplane you can get to America in only sixteen hours. Do you
think it's true?"

John still sits and talks. "No, I won't get married," he says,
continuing some private argument I have not followed. "I'll save
up and buy a motor-bike instead. And I'll ride very fast and I'll
never have any wife to fuss about being dangerous."

He has never been down again to visit me any evening since.
He was disappointed perhaps to find no-one but me and nothing
at all going on. Or perhaps it was only the mystery which drew
him down, unwilling but curious, and he really prefers his bed.
As for Peter, he grows at last more peaceful, less exhausted by
his London day, so that he falls asleep more easily now, and I
think he very seldom hears Big Ben strike nine o'clock, either on
the wireless or faintly in at his window when the nights are warm
and the wind is in the south.

Certainly to-night they are both asleep, for I went up to their
rooms an hour ago to close their windows because the rain was
blowing in. They both lay still without stirring, remote, withdrawn, as if in sleep they returned to some mysterious centre of
their being where no-one else could follow.

And I thought how self-composed they looked as they slept,
how proud almost. For these are the privileged young of Homo
sapiens, the paragon of animals, the conqueror of the world:
lordly creatures taking their rest in perfect safety, careless
and confident even in this defenceless oblivion. They both lie
sprawled at their ease, indifferent to noises and interruptions, to
people who come in and look at them and brush past the bed to
close the window. No atavistic dread of enemies in the night
troubles their sense of perfect security. They lie in peace and
dignity, no longer childish when they lie still like this, but of evi-
dent human status. And looking at Peter's sleeping face, with-

drawn now and untroubled, I think how it is not in sleep that children are pathetic, but when they are awake; being so vulnerable, so quickly moved to hope or disappointment, so wracked by grief or bewilderment, sensitive living creatures so easily and so dreadfully hurt.

But in sleep they lie at peace, as the dead do. And I remembered a film I once saw of refugees escaping in terror as war overtook them, stumbling, trampling, pushing each other ruthlessly aside to get a yard ahead, until suddenly the fire of a machine gun swept along the struggling file of wretched human creatures, turning their misery to screaming chaos. And a young women the camera had been watching for us was suddenly shot through the head and killed. Suddenly in all that horror she lay back utterly at peace. Remote, inviolate, safe. Her child might scream with terror beside her, the wounded all around her groan in agony, the air drown to a dark chaos of suffering and fear, but she was safe. Suddenly and blessedly safe. Rescued by death. I remember still the flooding relief as I looked at her peaceful face. No matter what happened, nothing again could ever trouble her, she was invulnerable at last. Only the living can be hurt.

I stood for a long time looking at the children, in sleep no longer familiar but enigmatic as strangers. And so they are strangers—these children I have lived with ever since they were born —growing up in this household as trees grow where they are planted because they have no choice, but yet grow mysteriously by their own unknown laws, as these children do too. For parents and home are the familiar soil and climate the new life must develop in, but the growing itself is mysterious always, and follows in each separate human being some different pattern we cannot understand.

And I thought how we can help them in their growth or hinder them by the things we do to them from the outside, but never change their essential inborn nature. We cannot, by anything we do, change them in a positive way to a different sort of creature.

We can stunt them certainly, prevent the growth they are capable of, twist and distort them. But we cannot put anything there which is not there already, we can only foster and encourage their possibilities, give them a chance to grow. For sycamores cannot be changed into oak trees however young we catch them, no matter how we treat them while they are growing. All we can do is produce at the end a good or a bad sycamore tree.

And I thought how strange it is that these two children of the same parents should be so very different, not only from both of us but also from each other. As if crossing a red flower with a white had produced, not two pinks as we might expect, but a blue and a yellow. And though they have grown up together with only a year between them, have been treated exactly alike as if they were twins, yet John and Peter are so completely different that no-one meeting them separately would ever guess they were brothers.

I watched them curiously for a long time, feeling how mysterious a human being is, even the simplest. And how the great difference is not between any one particular person and another, but between any one of us and the rest of creation. That the essential mystery is our new human consciousness, our intellectual conception of a world outside ourselves. And I thought how even these two young children are two worlds of awareness which have never existed before, and which no-one else can ever know. I looked at their faces as they lay there asleep in front of me, but their minds withdrawn and far-off on strange dark journeys where no-one can follow. And I stood so long that the last grey twilight faded in the windows, and their motionless heads blurred to a dim smudge on the pillow. And when I turned away and went to look, the night was clear again with the moon sailing, and I left the windows open because the rain was over.

IN THE YEAR OR MORE SINCE WE CAME TO LON-
don we have all grown so used to our life here together that
we can no longer remember the many things we once found
strange. But the house I do remember: the house was very odd.
We could none of us settle down to living in it.

It was not simply that our lives were in a new setting, for that
one soon gets used to, allotting new rooms to old activities, arranging the furniture to suit accustomed habits. We had put our
favourite chairs as we liked them, and our books on the shelves;
there were lamps by all the beds, our clothes and belongings in
drawers and cupboards. The house was arranged to live in, but
still we could not settle down.

A household is more than a house arranged, it is a house and
family united. And we were not united at all, we were awkward
together. The house was a very nice brick-box, and we no doubt
were good enough bricks, but we had not discovered the proper
way to fit us together: the bricks did not lie comfortably in the
box. In the first months we were never properly at home anywhere except in the kitchen, and the kitchen never counts. It is
so much the heart of any house that nothing disturbs its essential

life. If the kitchen is dead, then the whole house is no more than half-alive. So the domestic life of the kitchen survived all transplanting, but in the other rooms we were not at home, we were only visitors.

We would go and sit down with our books or letters, would settle ourselves for the evening, but sooner or later we drifted away—went to fetch some more coffee or look for the paper—and never came back.

Nor was it only the humans who were unsettled, restless and wandering, but in some strange way the house was uneasy too. We did not get on together: there was something wrong with the arrangement. And at last I found out what it was.

This house was built in the middle of the eighteenth century as a largish town-house for a prosperous family with servants. There are hundreds of houses like it all over London, a little larger or smaller but all similar, town-houses built to a recognized pattern to fit exactly a well-understood way of life. The servants—half a dozen or so I should think there were—lived and worked in the basement and the mews at the back. The ground-floor was arranged for meals, and for receiving strangers in a room near the door at the front of the house looking over the street. The drawing-room, as most important, took the whole of the first-floor space, an enormous room, stretching from back to front of the house, with tall windows, and marble fire-places and pillars, and elaborate plaster-work on walls and ceiling. It was large enough for a ball, but for family living could be divided by sliding doors between the pillars to make two separate rooms. Up above were three floors of bedrooms, two for the family, and the top floor for servants high up under the roof.

But the drawing-room was the centre of the household life, the place where the family sat about and gossiped, where friends were brought up when they called, and guests were entertained with more or less formality. It was the proper civilized setting for the sociable town-life of an eighteenth-century household.

The First Three Years Transplanted

Now, two centuries later, this house, which was built as a whole to fit a definite way of living, is divided up in slices to hold five different families. The caretaker lives in the basement, we have the first two floors, and the floors above are three more flats for three more separate households.

The ground-floor is not much changed except to make us a kitchen from a room which was once a library, but the first-floor drawing-room has disappeared completely, its imposing proportions divided into bedrooms with new low ceilings to suit the new small rooms and cover the broken-up plaster-work of the ceilings behind. Not that the rooms are particularly small, indeed they are still enormous by London-flat standards: they could still be divided again and leave plenty of room for the swinging of cats. But in the space of the old drawing-room they are no more than boxes packed close together, mere cupboards for sleeping where couples used to dance. Above my head as I lie in bed, but invisible now behind the new plain ceiling, I know there is a plaster relief of musical instruments, flutes and harps and fiddles bound together most elegantly I remember, with fluttering bows of ribbon.

By drawing-room standards we are squalidly domestic, for there is a bathroom now in the middle of the dance-floor, and a great gap where the new staircase climbs up from the hall below. The pillars have gone, and only in one bedroom is there still the carved marble fire-place and the elaborate plaster panels on the walls. There is nothing left of the old formality but the enormous windows in every room from floor to ceiling, looking urbanely out on the world through the railings of their balconies beyond.

The drawing-room, so one would think, is dead. But I wonder. The eighteenth century has a strong personality, and the architects were quite clear about how these houses were to be lived in. But can anyone build into the very bricks and mortar of a house the sense of the life for which the rooms are intended? If afterwards we come along with our undignified ways, and divide up the drawing-room into bedrooms, will they not then be bedrooms simply? Places to sleep in?

Certainly I arrived with my own quite definite idea of how to arrange the house. I knew what I intended just as clearly as the builder knew his plans at the start. The first floor was bedrooms I thought: we would sleep and bath and dress upstairs and come down to live our day-time lives on the ground-floor, as in any other house. Downstairs there was a fine large sitting-room with all we needed, alcoves for bookshelves, low tables for cups and papers and glasses, lights for reading, and comfortable chairs to sit and talk. But I reckoned without the house.

It was the first floor they built for that kind of living, not the rooms at ground-level; and despite all our mutilations the first floor still attracts the life it was meant for: we all tend to live in the bedrooms.

Somehow in those first months, without anyone quite knowing how or when, things made their way upstairs—flowers and books and reading-lamps, and even easy-chairs. All kinds of things appeared in the bedrooms as if of their own accord. I wondered sometimes if I should meet them at night on the staircase climbing up by themselves like the furniture in the Maupassant story. And we too, instead of sitting downstairs where we were meant to, would find ourselves on the first floor, strolling about with cups of coffee, sitting uncomfortably at the dressing-table writing letters, or watching the people in the street below from the sociable floor-length windows. We would sit on each other's beds and exchange the news of the day, the children would run off upstairs as soon as they finished their homework. We were settling in at last.

At first I resisted this double pattern of living in the same house. I disliked our vague migrations and never knowing where anyone would be. We were disorientated, I thought, by the moving in, and our family life would never be peaceful unless we got over these wandering ways.

But of course I was wrong. Family life grows like a plant to fit its new pot, and arranges its roots for itself without our interference. And in any case the conventions of the house are much stronger and far more persistent than my not very conventional housekeeping. We have accepted now the inbuilt atmosphere of the different rooms—ground floor for visitors, first floor for family affairs. We have settled down without conscious arrangement to a comfortable compromise within the new mould. There are bookshelves now in the bedrooms as well as downstairs, tall plants in pots stand on the floor of the window embrasures, there are chairs and desks and reading-lamps upstairs as well as down. The house has won. When a friend one day brought me roses, and I carried the bowl upstairs to the bedroom without thinking, then I realized that the spirit of the old drawing-room was with us for good as a determined resident ghost, settled contentedly perhaps between the two bedroom ceilings.

It is a pattern which gives our lives here a peculiar double quality. Downstairs is slightly formal. Walking down the staircase we enter a world which is halfway between private family life and the sociable life of the town outside. When we are on the ground floor we are tidy. We are properly dressed and ready to go out when we want to. The things we do on the ground floor are not intimate things: we are not taken unawares by callers who ring the bell, by passing acquaintances or strangers arriving unannounced from time to time to see us about this or that. The ground floor is the proper setting for the working life of an urban doctor's household.

But upstairs we do the kind of things I imagine all the people who have lived here before us were generally doing when servants took back word to unexpected callers that "Madam was not at home." We wash our hair and lounge about and gossip: have baths and change our clothes and wander about half-dressed. William lies at ease on the bed for half an hour with the newspaper, to recover from the rush of the day. I do my sewing upstairs, spread out lengths of cloth on the bed, cut them up into shapes, and sew them on the sewing-machine on the table in Peter's bedroom, making them into dresses and curtains and covers for chairs. I keep all the mess up there out of the way, the spilt pins and ends of cotton and snippets of cloth all over the floor. And the children live upstairs entirely, except for meals and homework. They bang about the bedrooms, and play water-games in the bath, and make dusty constructions of boxes and cardboard which balance by their beds and must not be touched. The floors of their rooms are littered with games which *please* will I leave when I clean the rooms? It's *most* important.

There is a great deal more going up and down stairs than there is in ordinary houses, for although invited guests are entertained at ground level, when close friends call we always sooner or later seem to find ourselves upstairs. When I hear the children thumping up the staircase with some new companion brought home for the first time, I know that they have accepted each other already and are friends.

Peter and John now are thoroughly at home in their new London life. Confident and cheerful they survey with satisfaction this wonderful enlargement of their small familiar universe. Yet in this first year they have suffered storms in plenty. They have wakened crying in the night, or felt ill in the morning only to escape some ordeal in the day ahead, or arriving home from school have collapsed in tears of relief on the doorstep as soon as I opened the door. But the worst is over now. Such storms as still beset them from time to time are no more than passing clouds in showery weather. They have won all kinds of battles this last year, and most of them without my help. For children once settled and confident can mostly be left it seems, to manage their difficulties without us. Only what we must do, always and un-alterably, is hold their hand firmly in general goodwill, then they themselves seem to deal with their own particular troubles far better than we can. In any case we do not know how to help them in any more definite way. We understand children, whether we realize it or not, only in terms of ourselves: we uncon-sciously consider them as grown-ups *manqués*. And children are not undeveloped versions of adult people: they are a different race of beings: they are children. Their troubles are not ours any more than their physical ailments. We have our own adult ills to suffer, but not their childish teething and chicken-pox and measles, and our adult ailments do not help us to understand theirs, nor how we should treat them.

Wise doctors I notice, merely put spotty children to bed and leave them to get well by themselves; and we too no doubt, knowing even less of their minds than the doctor knows of their bodies, do best to let them manage their troubles alone without our blind interference. We must only be kinder to them while they are in trouble, more patient and affectionate, as if we emo-tionally put them to bed as an empirical treatment for all their ills, without exact diagnosis. And luckily young children are astonishingly resilient. They seem to get over their difficulties as they get over their measles: we need only keep them in general good health and their childish constitution deals with the details as it deals with the spots.

No doubt their remedies for trouble are childish—charms and fancies and superstitions to ward off fear—but their minds are childish too, and these, no doubt, are the remedies they need. Our adult logic is no use to them, we cannot help, or even understand what is the matter. There is a street perhaps, which frightens them. For no reason at all that we can see, they feel it obscurely sinister, so that evil lurks behind half-open doors and crouches at corners to catch them. It is an ordeal they dread every day to walk along it to school. We may know quite well it is only an ordinary street and harmless as any other, but it is no use our saying so, no use insisting there is nothing to be afraid of. They know very well there is something, or why would they be afraid? It is only that grown-ups are blind and deaf and understand nothing.

Yet they seem to manage their fear for themselves if only we stay by them. They walk always perhaps on special safe squares of the pavement, or clutch in their pocket a certain blue marble they carry always as a magic charm to guard against all such mysterious unsubstantial foes. And the charm will work, as our logic can never work against such illogical enemies. The magic will keep them safe, will become a confident ritual—almost a game—and the unknown horror will grow tame and familiar. Until one day, rushing home perhaps in a hurry with news from school, they will forget the charm and forget the horror. They will run down the dreadful street unheeding—and nothing will happen. And afterwards they will remember, and know that it is over and there is nothing to fear any more. They will have fought their imagined monster with imagined weapons, and far more clearly than they could ever see by the light of our adult reasoning, they will see that it was all a little absurd; the terrors which once were horribly real will become a half-delightful game like the dragon in a pantomime. And they, not us, will be the dragon-tamers, the victors confident to face fresh trials. For we all have to do our own growing-up: there is no way, alas, to be wise by proxy. It is a long and difficult journey from magic to reason, and children must make it for themselves, at their own intellectual pace, a step at a time. If we hurry them they will only stumble, and if we carry them over the difficult parts they will only flounder helplessly later on when the road gets rough again and we are not there to help them. Unless we have measles when we are young we are not immune later on. But parents cannot help, I think, any more than doctors. We can only stay patiently by them and wait for them to get better.

In any case young children can seldom explain their ordeals to anyone else. Nor I think do they wish to even if they could. Their troubles are secret and not to be exposed to the alien air of adult reason. Often their chance remarks are astonishingly revealing, but it is by accident and not intent. They tell us almost nothing of their own free will, and I think our adult need to communicate is not one of the needs of children. They are too completely self-centred to think in terms of other people.

So I know very little of what has happened to Peter and John in this last year in London: only that at first they were anxious and now they are not. They are over their mental measles as they are over too most of the spotty diseases of childhood. But that, they feel, is no real benefit, for being ill they consider one of the pleasures of life.

As doctor's children Peter and John enjoy one great advantage—not an advantage they can be expected to appreciate, but a real one none-the-less. It is not that they have constant medical care, nor expert advice for their slightest ailment. Not at all. The advantage is something quite different. It is that no-one ever fusses in the very least about their health. It is taken for granted, and well is left alone. As far as they are concerned they are perfectly well unless they are taken properly ill: there is no inbetween state of fuss. And illness is perfectly simple and well-defined. Illness is fever, illness is bed, illness is sooner or later spots. Spotty or well. There is nothing else.

From time to time of course, they tell me they feel ill. But the rules are very simple. If they have a temperature they are put to bed. If they have no temperature they are well. It is not the least use complaining of a headache when they must do something they do not like, or saying their throat is sore when they do not much fancy the look of the day ahead. All such minor woes I treat in a brisk hearty fashion which must be infuriating. "What you need," I tell them cheerfully, "is a nice hot bath and early to bed." If they are really out-of-sorts they are glad to be bustled off so efficiently, but when they are well they detest both bath and bed. It is a treatment quite wonderfully effective for curing the whole vast range of imagined ailments.

If they are to be considered as serious invalids, then they must first produce a temperature, and if possible a good high temperature which is still there next morning. Then the results are well worth suffering for. The invalid is fussed and cossetted and generally made much of; helped undress and put to bed with extra pillows and unlimited orange-juice. They lend each other their dearest treasures in love and sympathy. And if the temperature is high enough and lasts long enough to count as really ill, that is the best of all. For then everyone who passes their door must look in to greet them, if only to smile; and everyone who goes out of the house must bring back some present however small. A postcard will do, or an apple to polish on their pillow, or a bundle of rubber bands or a roll of cellotape—for these are the working necessities of small boys' lives and they never have enough. Even when they are too ill to use them, they still like to keep them under their pillow as a treasured hoard for the future. And in case I am not going out, I keep a special locked cupboard full of small presents which I collect when I see them in shops, and hide away for Christmas stockings and these sessions in bed which are part of the yearly rhythm in the lives of all small children.

This business of being properly ill is a condition so immensely desirable that I wonder it does not turn them into a pair of hypochondriacs. Perhaps it might if it were not so difficult for a healthy child to produce a temperature at will, or even to stay in bed for long without one. But it is a sweetly-privileged state, and John in particular hankers after it from time to time. He grows bored perhaps when his week is uneventful, or knows that to-morrow he is in for trouble at school (for John is often in trouble). He feels, no doubt, how pleasant it would be to stay

at home and have us all make much of him, instead of going off
to school to be dealt with. So he persuades himself he perhaps
feels ill, finds the thermometer in the kitchen drawer, and sits
with it hopefully in his mouth for as long as ten minutes together,
trying to work it up just an extra fraction so that it can count as
ill. Peter and I come and tease him to make him giggle, and tell
him silly stories to make him explode with laughter. We ask him
questions we know he is longing to answer, so that he gesticulates
in the most extraordinary dumb-show rather than open his lips
the slightest chink to let in a draught of cold air and send the
thermometer down again.

I was the last of us to be ill enough for bed, and though it was
only influenza, still my temperature was high enough to qualify
for the full ceremonial treatment. I have never in all my life been
so visited as I was while I lay in bed, never been brought so
much news of the town. For the others were all energetically
healthy. We never seem to catch the same ailments; we are all of
us ill when we are ready, each in his own good time, and not
because anyone else in the house is ailing. Medically we seem the
most independent of families.

So the children came and sat on my bed, thoroughly impressed
by the soaring heights I could reach on the thermometer in a
mere half-minute without any effort at all. They were faintly
complacent too, that *I* should be in bed I suppose, and not them
for a change; for they had never seen me take to my bed before,
and rôles reversed are always a piquant amusement.

They treated me with the greatest kindness, rushing up to see
me as soon as they came into the house, bringing saved snippets
of news and accounts of the world outside. I have never been
told so much about school as I was while I lay in bed too feverish
to want anything but leaving alone to die in peace without so
much interruption.

But they were delighted that they knew so well the rules for
sickrooms, knew exactly what was expected of the rest of the

household when anyone was in bed. They brought me presents, toffees and bunches of flowers and—what else could they bring? They must have been puzzled, for grown-ups are difficult, having no liking for toys. Housekeeping is my game, so the children seem to think, and they went to their favourite Woolworth's on the way home from school to find me household presents.

"I've got you a new little screw-driver with a nice blue handle." And Peter took it out of its paper bag and laid it on the bedclothes over my stomach. "But do you know how expensive *tea-spoons* are?" He had evidently explored areas of Woolworth's which he must always till then have considered my private household territory. "Tea-spoons are one and six. One and six *each!* I think it's *awful*. Are they always as expensive as that?"

But John arrived beaming and breathless. "I've brought you a present. It's what you like," so he confidently assured me. And beside the blue screw-driver he put down a box of drawing-pins with brightly-coloured heads. He is quite right: it is just what I do like. I like the drawing-pins I use to have coloured tops and not made of brass going rusty, as John must have noticed and approved.

Mostly though, it was books I was brought, and constant showers of newspapers. He was going to the library, William said, so what would I like?

That is always easy—I would like a smart West-End novel. For ever since William overheard a woman at the library, it has been one of our favourite family definitions. Could the librarian recommend a book she would like? the woman wanted to know. But what sort *did* she like? the librarian most reasonably asked. Oh, said the woman, what she liked best was a smart West-End novel.

It is what we all like of course, especially when we are ill in bed, but alas there are not enough, not *nearly* enough however often we reread *The Golden Bowl* and *Mrs. Dalloway* and *The Death of the Heart* and Ronald Firbank's fancies. But what William came back with was not a novel at all, but a *History of Witchcraft* with illustrations, and another volume of even more doubtful value for the sick-room called *Canons of Giant Art— Twenty Torsos in Heroic Landscapes*. I wonder if it was really as extraordinary as I remember? Or was part of the oddness perhaps, the effect of a soaring temperature? But certainly I have got the title right, for I looked at it weakly for hours on the table by my bed, and the title alone is surely peculiar.

Well, he would go to Bumpus's, William said, feeling perhaps that the books of his choice looked less tempting by my bed than they did on the library shelves. He would go and buy me something new.

But because he chooses presents as they tell us we should, William chooses always what he would like for himself. And because what he likes is what he is used to, he chooses always the books we have got already. For he is absent-minded, and will not believe what I tell him—that if he is drawn to a book on the shelves of the shop, it is only because he is used to seeing it on his own shelves at home; and that if I packed up all his books and sent them on ahead of him to be scattered about the bookshop, he would pick them out again unerringly and bring them all safely back home.

"I've brought you a present," he says, giving me the parcel to unpack for myself (unlike the children). "I hope we haven't got it already." He is less confident now, watching me undo the string. And as I unfold the paper, doubt overwhelms him. As well it might.

"They said you could change them if you wanted," he says with a rueful air, watching my face.

For we always have got them already. Sometimes, when he brings them from shops too far off to go back and change them, we already have them twice. We have three copies of the *Little*

Guide to Sussex. There used to be four, but we managed to give one away to some friends who most obligingly bought a house on the Sussex coast.

But influenza was long ago, an almost forgotten interlude of the dark winter weather. Nor, despite the family's attentions, did I really enjoy it with the children's whole-hearted enthusiasm. Too many things go wrong when the housekeeper is away, the boys grow bad-tempered in their unexpected independence, and at tea-time they quarrel unless I am there—as today I am urgently reminded by a furious double ring on the door-bell. For this is not the postman ringing twice, but Peter home from school in a temper.

They have lived in the town now long enough to manage alone in the traffic, but they still arrive home irritable from the tension of noise and bustle and too-many people: and today, as they often do, they have quarrelled again on the bus. It is not that they find each other any more tiresome than most brothers do, but at this age children quarrel with irritation, as younger children are sick with excitement.

"I hate John." It is a burst of fury from Peter who has come back alone. "I *hate* him," he says, slinging his satchel violently across the kitchen. "I shall never speak to him again. *Never.*" So he declares with angry satisfaction. "I shall write it down in my diary so that I don't forget. There's a special page for things like that" (he is growing calmer now). "It's called Memorandum. There's a special page for nearly everything—like what size shoes you take, and what time there's a train." His voice has changed from furious through impersonal to a contented note of pleasure, for already he is forgetting the quarrel in the delights of his diary. And he has not even made a note for himself under Memorandum.

"It's a *wonderful* diary. It tells you everything you ever want to know. Like when there's an eclipse, and how fast horses can run, and how many miles it is round the world." For Peter likes facts, no matter what, the more the better.

"Pigeons fly faster than eagles. Did you know?" He is peaceful now in the peaceful house, John's tiresomeness forgotten, and the trying world shut out behind him on the doorstep.

"Coming back from school I saw a hole in the road, and I looked inside for you. And in the bottom was lots and lots of round pebbles like at the sea-side." For Peter encourages my interests as I do his, and I have always been curious about holes in roads. I like to know what kind of earth is buried below the pavement I walk on—clay or sand or gravel. I like to see what goes on underneath, and whether the hole will fill with underground water like a well. Then there are all kinds of problems which have occupied me ever since I too was a child. Will the soil be wet because it cannot dry out through the lid of roads and buildings? or dry because the rain never reaches it? And how do trees live, growing through tiny holes in the pavement where no rain ever gets to their roots?

These are preoccupations which the children consider perfectly sensible, far more sensible than most of the things which interest grown-up people. "Grown-ups talk," I overheard John declare with scorn one day. "They don't play games or do anything when they meet each other. They just *talk*. For hours and hours. And they don't even talk about interesting things like asking riddles or arranging secret societies." But holes in the ground are included in the "interesting things," and whenever they see one they look into it for me, and report when they get back home.

John has come in now, smiling airily and talking of other things, so that I know the quarrel on the bus was mostly his fault, and he has loitered up the street from the bus-stop on purpose to give Peter's fury time to die down. He was wise, for Peter glares at him, but swallows down whatever he meant to say, and they settle at the table for tea together as if nothing had happened.

Their quarrels are not always as mild or as quickly over as this, though I try always not to interfere, since I can see that boys of this age have a dogs-delight-to-bark-and-bite side of their nature which it is useless to suppress. Like holding a finger on the end of a hosepipe, the water will only spurt out more violently somewhere else. Peter and John are always ready to fight when they come in at tea-time. A crowded school day has ended in a struggle home through rush-hour crowds on rush-hour buses, and once safely in the calm familiar kitchen their pent-up irritation explodes in an emotional belch and afterwards leaves them peaceful.

So I take no notice of their minor dog-fights and only keep out of the way till they have settled down. Even so, I should have known better than to give them at tea-time any excuse for quarrelling. I should have known what would happen when I gave them a box of coloured pencils to share out between them, and left them to choose for themselves the colours they wanted. Their bickering I ignored, and the usual thump and clatter of boys, but hearing their shouting voices change to quiet fury, and the more-or-less benevolent scuffling turn to a silent struggle, I knew that the dog-fight was becoming far too much like the cats of Kilkenny and it was time for me to intervene.

I separated them, scolded them, sat them apart at opposite ends of the table and divided the pencils into equal shares. But they both sat glowering, mutinous still and dissatisfied, glaring sullenly at each other, sitting tense on the edge of their chairs ready to fight again as soon as I was safely out of hearing.

"All right," I asked. "What would *you* do if *you* were the mother?"

"O well," said Peter, suddenly relaxed and cheerfully grinning, his irritation as completely gone as the switching off of a motor. "O well. That's different. If *we* were the mother we'd divide the pencils in two halves and give us one each. And if either of us said *one single word* of argument, we'd throw the *whole lot* on the fire straight away."

John beamed his agreement, and they leaned back happily on their chairs in perfect accord with each other, delighted with their god-like wisdom as parents-to-be. For they not only accept the established discipline, but approve of it impartially. They seem to have decided that on the whole my household management is a fair and efficient system, however much they may enjoy grumbling about the details from time to time.

But John looks at me shrewdly and speculatively. Certainly this is a confidential moment, but even so he must not trespass too far over the necessary boundary between parents and children. Then deciding that today it is safe, "But we know *you* wouldn't throw them on the fire, Dardy, unless we made you *really* cross. And if we did we'd stop quarrelling just in time."

I always suspected that they would be far stricter than I am, being too young to be troubled by kindness of heart. For unless they upset me, or provoke me by deliberate defiance, I hate to punish them. Which they both know perfectly well, and I daresay they think less of me for my half-hearted methods, only respecting the real disciplinarian, as children do. Still they have got to learn sometime that grown-ups are not the rational logical creatures they may once have imagined, but that we too have our moods and inconsistencies which they must learn to manage as we do theirs.

However, I suspect I am preaching to the already well-converted, and that they can foresee my behaviour far more clearly than I can foresee theirs, since for so many years I have been the absolute tyrant who governed their lives, and had to be understood before they could manage me. For manage me they do, with shrewdness and affection; and far more often, I have no doubt at all, than I ever suspect. For besides being tiresome small boys, which is mostly their ages, they are both of them reasonable people, and mostly do as I say without argument, to please me because we are friends. But although they may make deliberate judgements with adult detachment, they are overwhelmed still, as soon as they are in any way disturbed, by the same old irrational childish emotions.

Like all children they are intensely interested in each other's ages; age, for children, being a universally accepted hierarchy. For them quite simply age is merit; so that an older child is considered a perfectly natural superior, is expected to be wiser, braver, stronger, better in every way than his younger fellows. His birthday may be only a week or two before theirs, but no matter—he is older and therefore better. There is no disputing dates. I can see that it gives us grown-ups a quite impossible start, since we are all of us so immeasurably old already.

The first question young children ask each other, before even they ask for names, is how old they are. And the answer is always prompt and exact—not seven or eight, but seven and a quarter or eight and five months. It is a fact of the very greatest importance, and they must feel themselves changing and growing up at bewildering speed for a month to make so vast a difference. To fight someone younger than oneself is to be a bully, for size seems of much less importance than birthdays. All children younger than themselves John and Peter regard with a kindly condescension.

"You mustn't mind. He can't help it. It's only because he's so young," they told me in tolerant excuse for a schoolfriend who came to stay one week-end, a self-possessed small boy with courtly manners as formal and exquisite as a sea-shell. He must, I suppose, be a month or so younger even than John, or they would not both feel so protective towards him. For although he played happily and noisily all day, chattered politely at meals, splashed and giggled in the bath, and bounced and giggled in bed; yet when I said "Good night, and go to sleep now," I was scarcely downstairs before the house echoed with his heart-broken sobbing, muffled for decency's sake in the pillow, but a dreadful insistent rhythm which summoned me running back upstairs to his bed.

ME: Dear Christopher. Whatever's the matter?

CHRISTOPHER: Nothing's the matter, thank you very much.

Clearly he was not going to tell me and I should have to guess.

ME: Is it because John's been unkind?

For a lot of scuffling and grunting went on in their pillow-fight.

CHRISTOPHER: No. John's been very kind thank you. He's given me his engine.

It is a conversation carried on on his side in the most polite of voices between great gulping sobs, and I am fascinated to watch the two planes side by side, the urbane young visitor and the homesick child.

ME: Is it because you don't like it here at night?

CHRISTOPHER: No. I like it very much thank you.

I can scarcely make out the words between the sobs, more uncontrollable now, so that I can guess I am getting nearer the trouble.

ME: Is it because it isn't your own bed that you're used to?

CHRISTOPHER: Yes, it is.

And the bed shakes and rocks to enormous and dreadful sobbing. "But I don't know why I'm crying," he says as soon as he can, and after all he can scarcely be expected to understand about the two separate planes.

ME: Would you like me to put you in the car—just like that in your red pyjamas (there is a giggle through the sobs) and take you straight back to your own bed this minute?

CHRISTOPHER: No thank you. I'd like to stay here. It doesn't matter about crying.

But it does matter. I cannot bear it. Even to please him I cannot stand it another moment.

ME: Well would you like John to come and sleep with you?

CHRISTOPHER: Yes please, I would.

There is a final gasping gulp and a great deal of nose-blowing, and he sits up sociably in bed to welcome his visitor. John comes running in at once (for of course he was listening), his sympathetic concern changed now to delight at this quite unlooked-for development. As to how much sleep they got in the end, I should not like to guess. But it surely must be better to giggle half the night than to sob, and after all he is only young, so he really can't help it, as my superior old children keep on insisting.

Whether or not they also understand about the need for one's own bed at night, that I have no way of knowing. For if they too sob themselves to sleep when they go away alone to other people's houses, then they do it quietly and no-one has noticed. And certainly they would never tell me themselves: they are far too old, and would be ashamed.

To face the world, soft snails need their shells to protect them, and we are all of us snails and defenceless like Christopher when we are stripped of the shell of our own familiar lives. For the world outside is dreadful with great melancholy convictions, the knowledge of suffering and fear and loneliness and death, with indefinable misgivings which possess our defenceless spirits, the universal sorrows which beset all living creatures.

There are moods when it is horrible that we must die as animals die and trees, when it is fearful to remember that always, just beyond our vision, there waits the unending night which will engulf us at last. Against the dark we have no defence but the circle of candlelight which is our small familiar life, and when this frail light wavers for any reason—in sudden disaster, or menacing sickness, or only perhaps moving house or changing schools—it is then that we know with dread how defenceless we are against despair. Poor Christopher, to brave such terrors only by going away for the week-end.

It is a sense of vague fear which young children must know far more often and more suddenly than we do, since they are strangers in so many places. It is why, I suppose, they need us so desperately for their background—not our attention, nor our indulgence, nor even particularly our incidental kindnesses, but need our presence simply: steady, benevolent, familiar: a haven in strange seas. But we all of us need from time to time some comfortable shelter, some small area which we can encompass with affection and wall round with blindness; and when we go beyond it we still take with us for protection the conciousness of our refuge. For we are not free-ranging god-like minds to sail untroubled over the wide seas, we are small and human and easily hurt, and even the toughest need now and then in trouble some consciousness of shelter. Alone we are lost. It is easy to see why men have made gods for their comfort.

"But God is a preacher who preaches to himself," so John told me one day, a mysterious and symbolic-sounding pronouncement. Once or twice lately John has made such unexpected comments, and I can only suppose that Divinity has been seriously added to the three R's at school; though even so, John's idea of God is scarcely more decorous than last year's portrait of Jesus. But I suppose for young children where everything is new and still-to-be-learned, nothing can yet seem incongruous. Only in the domestic world they know can anything strike them as absurd. The attributes of God they accept as whatever we choose to tell them, but it would never do, they would shout with protest, if I gave them porridge for tea instead of breakfast, or if William went off to hospital absent-mindedly in his pyjamas. This household life is their snail-shell as it is mine too, and is most women's I suppose. It is why, moving to London with my domestic world still to establish, I was so uncomfortably vulnerable to the disquiet which haunts big cities. For cities have their own moods of darkness, more violent than country melancholy, more fierce and sudden. Yet the fears which beset us in cities are vague and difficult to account for. Partly perhaps it is the sense of strange worlds around us, the

> *"Blank misgivings of a creature*
> *Moving about in worlds not realised."*

For Wordsworth's misgivings is a better word than fear. It is not fear exactly, nor anything so definite. It is not even anxiety. We have no reason to suppose that these unrealized worlds are hostile. Yet still we are troubled by a consciousness of hungry generations, relentless and indifferent. It is terrible that people should pass us by, talking to their companions, as if we were invisible. For it is the indifference above all which is frightening: that in this strange place we have nowhere we belong, no friends, no life which has any part in this society of preoccupied strangers. If we falter, no-one will help us, not because they wish us ill, but simply because they have not noticed our existence, we are no concern of theirs. It is a mood which lurks in all big cities to engulf the defenceless, those who have no busy life of their own to carry them unnoticing over the bottomless seas: a waiting despair which breathes on us chilly from the corners of streets, turning the sunshine to bright cold mockery, and sending us hurrying blindly to whatever shelter we can find.

For me it is not a personal trouble, but a consciousness of the dread which waits to swallow all strangers in strange places. Perhaps it is a compensating despair of all great cities, as if the gaiety which delights us in a metropolis were set in one side of a pair of scales, and because the scales must balance, the other side is heavy with these lurking indefinable fears; as if one must be paid for by the other. It is a mood of Paris which Baudelaire knew well, and for a stranger in Rome it becomes so savage a conviction that I would believe anyone who told me that the lonely there were left to die, or still thrown to the lions. And coming back to London after an absence, there is still for me a day of dismay before I am enclosed again in my London life like the walls of a bubble.

"It is a greater piece of skill," says a seventeenth-century writer on London, "to live in a populous place, where multitude of people reside, than in a solitary and private place among a few . . . the city being like a vast sea, full of gusts, fearful dangerous shelves and rocks, ready at every storm to sink and cast away the weak and unexperienced bark."

In this vast sea of London the children and I now have our harbours, as William has always had his own different world of medicine, a closely-linked community of shared work and knowledge and colleagues who all know each other. Though William I think needs his snail-shell less than any of us, being the naturally urban man. He breathes the city atmosphere as his native air, and the indifference which oppresses me, for him is freedom. He uses the city background confidently for his interest and entertainment, and in the country, after a day or two of quiet he is drawn always to the promise of the nearest town.

Yet I too hope in time to become a townee, since every so long we shed our old skin of living like a snake and come forth different creatures. It is a process which I hope will cease in time as I grow older, for like all changes it has its most uncomfortable growing-pains. Out in the open we see too clearly and without illusion. Until we are covered by our new skin we are dangerously vulnerable, over-sensitive to passing moods and disappointments.

But perhaps I shall stay a townee, and not go on changing into a traveller or a hermit or anything else equally unlikely. Perhaps soon I shall crystallize out and stay fixed at some half-way stage of being, part townee, part country-cousin: a double personality like the Kmer figure who was two gods united, and wore two different hair-styles, one on each side of his head. Like all Kmer gods he looks most wonderfully happy, and so would I be, passing at my pleasure from one life to the other, as if a familiar gangway carried me between ship and land, safely over the death by drowning which lies between. I would like to pass from town to country and back again as I pleased, like sharing the year between one's Summer and Winter Palaces. It has always seemed to me an ideal way of living.

D ARDY."
This is how John begins all conversations, by first
making contact with the person he wants to talk to. It is as if we
were speaking to each other over the telephone and he likes to be
sure I am there and listening before he begins.

JOHN: Dardy.

ME: Yes.

JOHN: You know that basin in the downstairs cloakroom?

ME: Yes.

JOHN: Well, do we often use it?

ME: Not very often.

JOHN: If you push the plug on hard does it keep the water in
for ever?

ME: Yes, I expect so. I've never tried.

JOHN: Well, do you think I could borrow it?

ME: It depends what for. What do you want to do?

I learned long ago from sad experience that I must never say
Yes to any of John's simple-sounding requests; that I must find
out first whether they were traps. For children are distressingly
unscrupulous. They will lure us into absent-minded statements
when we are busy with something else, and afterwards hold us
to our casual word as a sacred promise. They are utterly ruthless.

"You know you always keep promises. You *always* do, don't you?" They will appeal to the noblest of family principles to get their own way.

I used to think they did not trap us on purpose. But now I know better. I know that I must always find out very carefully just exactly what it is John wants to do before I say Yes to anything at all. Especially I must always be wary when he leads up to the subject with all this care and circumspection. Besides, how can he *borrow* a wash-basin?

"What do you want the wash-basin for?" I wait for him to answer. There is a long pause while he stares unseeing out of the window, then a sigh—profound, resigned, curiously adult. Whatever it is he wants to do in the wash-basin clearly sounds impossible when put into words. After the sigh there is another silence, then he says quietly in a subdued and rather plaintive voice, "I *would* like to have a pet in London."

This is the third year since we came to London, and this is the first I have heard of wanting any animal to adopt. (Though John calls it adpot—"It's what you do to orphans," he told me.)

He waits for me to answer, looking at me sorrowfully with wide blue eyes. He knows that if he is reasonable I am easily persuaded about most things, but on the other hand I am very difficult about pets. For I have had enough experience of his periodic enthusiasms for keeping animals to know that after the first week or two of enchantment he will take no more interest in whatever poor captive creature it is, and that I shall be left to feed it and clean it until I can bring myself to be firm enough to give it away. But always the idea of a new pet is as enticing as a new love affair, and in such matters we are all of us unwilling to learn from experience.

John is talking half to himself in a quiet hopeless voice. "At Harrods' Pet Shop they sometimes sell alligators. A boy at school told me so. And I thought just a very little one might fit in that downstairs wash-basin." But he says it sadly, without conviction.

Clearly this time he expects no answer, and he sighs again.

I can see now why he has been so curious lately about the habits of snakes and lion-cubs and koala-bears and so on. I thought it was only an interest in natural history after our week-end visits to the Zoo, but I can see now that it has been from the start something far more significant and sinister.

Indeed John's conversations are seldom simply on one level at once. His consciousness of other people's reactions is acute and complicated, and because he himself can manipulate several threads of thought and attention at the same time, he realizes that other people must be able to do so too. Our conversation is a manner of fencing, with the extra complication that we both pretend it is straightforward talk. What we really mean must be implied and deduced from what we say or do not say; by exactly how and when we change the subject.

But this time he seems to have decided for himself that an alligator is really too ambitious to hope for in the way of pets, and it seems kinder to talk of something else.

"What have you been doing at school to-day?" John realizes that the first round of our encounter is over and that he must approach me afresh from some new angle. He is perfectly cheerful about it.

"Well, we had a French lesson and I drew a picture. I'll show you, because it isn't finished and I've got to do it for Prep."

He rummages through his satchel and brings out a crumpled crayon drawing. It is a stylized family group of four people standing neatly in a row, with a cat at one end and a dog at the other. Underneath is written in a careful copy-book hand quite unlike his English writing:

> *Le père a un chien.*
> *La mère a un chat.*
> *Le père aime sa fille.*
> *La mère aime son fils.*
> *Le chat aime la fille.*

Goodness. Am I expected to work out this tangle of passions? I am always bewildered by such complicated emotional dramas, and this one is altogether too much like the plots of the modern psychological plays which I find so heavily indigestible. Only the dog, a sensible creature, has no part in this intricate web of passionate relationships. But in a modern play there would be no difficulty about *that*. The dog could be given a voice and made to comment on the action like a Greek chorus.

But that is not at all how John sees the dog. To John at the moment any animal is quite simply a desirable pet. Not that it is a dog he wants this time, for when we lived in the country he had a dog of his own, and a litter of puppies too, and took surprisingly little interest in any of them. Nor does he care about cats, for since he grew up with half-a-dozen or so as the normal mouse-hunting population of the farm, he no more considers a cat as a pet than he would a hen in the yard or a cow in the field. To John dogs and cats are mere farm animals, useful no doubt, but dull. He is thinking of something much less conventional and he is very persistent.

"I'm very glad my father's a doctor," he suddenly says in a satisfied voice.

"Are you? Why?" I ask, smugly expecting some praise of a fine profession. But I really should have known better. John and I are not at the moment conversing on those sort of terms; we are not exchanging civilities. Rather I am besieged by an agile and quick-witted opponent who will win in the end no doubt, simply because he cares more about getting into the fortress than I care about keeping him out.

"Well," says John triumphantly, delighted that I should fall so easily into his trap. "Well William's a doctor. So there's always someone in the house to answer the telephone when people get ill and ring up. So that if I got some canaries there'd always be someone to feed them when I'm away on holiday."

Canaries! This is the first I have heard of canaries. How

nimbly he changes his ground for attack. So all the time we have been talking about his French dog, he has been thinking about his English canaries, and planning in advance how he can forestall my probable objections. For John and I walk round each other as warily as wild animals. He is already my match at innuendo and *double-entendre*, and we are both well aware of each other's tactics. The only advantage I imagine I still have is that although I know perfectly well he manages me deliberately, I think he does not realize yet that I am conscious of his manoeuvres, but still supposes me a large and stupid fish to be cleverly played. When I swerve away from the thrusts of his argument he still supposes, or at least I hope he does, that my movements are merely chance and not deliberate dodging. But I dare say I am mistaken, and he probably realizes quite well that we are equal opponents in the fencing, for our children understand us far more shrewdly than we like to suppose.

Of course I could end it all by a blunt and final No. Sometimes I do. But how brutal and against all the rules of our game. One simply does not end fencing matches by producing a blunderbuss from behind one's back and hitting one's opponent on the head. However, unless I am prepared to go on with the fencing indefinitely I can see that sooner or later I shall have to admit some new animal to the family circle, for John is wearingly persistent. The only decision I shall insist on making myself is what kind of animal it shall be. For after all, I am the person it really concerns. I know quite well from pets of the past that I shall be the one who looks after it, either by supervising a grumbling John, or much more simply by doing it weakly myself. I know exactly how much trust I can put in his enthusiastic promise to do "every single thing myself, and this time you need never do anything at all. Absolutely *nothing*." And since I shall have to do absolutely everything, the animal has got to be something which needs the least possible attention. Certainly not hamsters, nor guinea-pigs, nor mice, nor any of the other creatures John fancies from time to time—active mammals all of them, and needing constant care. Fish are ideal of course, but John long since grew weary of the charms of goldfish in a tank, even though Peter encouraged him by growing exotic water-weeds in the sand at the bottom.

Peter's interests are rather with plants than animals, which is a relief, for plants are simpler to look after, and less disastrous when neglected. His bedroom window-sill is always messy with languishing cactuses, with mustard-and-cress growing in old sponges, and carrot-tops sprouting from saucers. This for Peter is an astonishing miracle, as it was for me, I still remember, in my city childhood. One simply found a likely-looking carrot in the vegetable box in the kitchen, sliced off the top and put it on a saucer with a little water. After a week or so on the window-sill it would send up, miraculously from nowhere, a circle of feathery leaves. I was enchanted always. Roses and lilies were very fine of course, but no more than one expected from reasonable rooted flowers—merest commonplace beside this Aaron's rod of a dead carrot-top, which without roots or soil but simply because I invited, would break out in this glad green fountain of leaves.

Peter too is entranced by this willingness to grow on a bare saucer, though I think he sees far fewer miracles than I did at his age, for Peter is a more rational creature than ever I was.

But acorns, I told him, will grow in the tops of bottles: an unlikely possibility which he none-the-less believes because I say it is so; and he balances on the sash of his window a row of little bottles full of water with acorns wedged in the necks. And in no more time, he thinks, than he will take to grow as high as my shoulder, his acorns will soar to great oak trees, wide and leafy, to hide King Charles from his enemies and shelter whole armies from the sun. By next year, he thinks, we shall have a forest on the bedroom window-sill.

So quite certainly I believed when I was Peter's age, and filled my city bedroom with growing things, longing for the country I had never known except during rare and far-too-quickly-over holidays. I had canaries too—two of them, which I tamed so that they would perch on my finger and eat from my hand the groundsel which I hunted for on patches of waste ground on the way home from school. And every spring there was a goldfish-bowl full of shadowy grey frog-spawn which I watched fascinated as the black spots uncurled, grew daily larger, developed to fierce carnivorous tadpoles, sprouted legs like roots and changed all too soon into tiny frogs. This was always a sad though intriguing stage, for although I kept the poor little things in a box of wet moss, with every comfort I could think of to make young frogs feel at home, they were constantly escaping. Every evening rushing home from school I would find the box empty, and search for the tiny creatures round the bedroom floor, sorrowfully, since each day some vanished forever, or perished miserably in the fluffy dust which seems to be a natural growth of the floors under all beds, no matter how often we sweep them.

But there is no need to encourage John with stories of frogs and tame canaries. He is both determined and enterprising, and needs no-one's help ever in arranging his own affairs. He has given me two letters to address and post for him, two recent birthday thank-you letters which he now writes for himself without my prompting. The first one is simple.

"Dear Godfather,
   thank you very much for the 6-part penknife it will be very usefull for cutting bows and arrows and splicing rope for climbing trees and opening tins and bottels as well as taking of the lids of trecal tins with love from John."

That can go into an envelope and off without trouble. But the second letter is a very different matter. It is a thank-you letter to a friend in Yorkshire, who does not know how potentially dangerous it is to give John money instead of penknives.

> "Thank you very much for the 10/- Dardy told me that up in Yorkshire there they are very good at breeding Canaryz so perhaps by any chance you might now someone who breeds nice hardy Canaryz? because I do so much want a pet of some sort that does not die when we put it in the kichin because it might die with the gas-stove with love from John."

It looks an urbane sort of letter, even though rather breathless since it lacks all punctuation. But I can see that it is really alarmingly single-minded, for he has neglected all the formulas he generally uses: things like "I hope you are getting on," and "I hope you are in the best of health"—a whole repertoire of phrases which he keeps for rounding off letters to his satisfaction. But this is no mere duty letter written to fill up the page of writing which I insist on for saying thank-you. This I recognize for what it is: a masterly move in our long guerilla warfare of Pets versus No Pets. I look at it doubtfully and wonder whether to post it without comment. And I remember John's last school report. "Conduct. Good when fully occupied. Out of class only fair." Then follow kinder things like "high-spirited and affectionate," but they are only sugar on the pill of John's general tiresomeness. "It is good for a school to have boys like John, even though he is a nuisance."

It seemed to me at the time, and it still does, a very cryptic assessment. Am I meant to understand that he is good for the household too? Perhaps he is, but I do not want to be done good to. It is too late; I am too old now for improvement. Besides I have been disciplined quite enough already, with country life and wartime and eight years of John's company. Quite certainly I need no more discipline of keeping pets. I hoped we had finished with them for good.

The First Three Years Transplanted

Yet I suppose it is a measure of the children's feeling at home here now that they are ready to make a home in their turn for some other bewildered creature. Not that they will do of course, for children are not really home-makers—or only now and then in sudden bouts of enthusiasm. And homes are not made by such fitful methods. To be any use, homes must be made conscientiously and every day alas, year in year out, as I have painstakingly discovered.

But I must decide what to do. I must make up my mind about the canaries. Do birds die in a kitchen with a gas-stove, I wonder? Does John really know? or is it only that he has noticed that the plants I grow on the kitchen window-sill are always sickly invalids, though all the other windows of the house are so luxuriantly leafy that I wonder sometimes if there will still be room for us as well in another year's time, or whether the plants will take over the house as a conservatory, and we shall all have to camp out in the yard with the vine.

Certainly I must find out about canaries and gas-stoves before we start, for pets which sicken and die are a domestic tragedy not lightly to be risked. It seems to make no difference that for months past the children have ignored them, forgotten to feed them or give them water, and never cleaned them out unless I insisted and supervised their grumbling incompetence. No matter—as soon as a pet is ill it becomes a focus of the intensest interest. It is lovingly tended, its progress is watched minute by minute, and its hour by hour condition for better or worse decides the emotional climate for the whole household in the most tiresome way. When a pet is ill no-one must laugh, not even William and I at the other end of the house. Cheerfulness, we are made to feel, is callous indifference. With sickness under our roof we must all behave like a funeral.

I suppose it is that the normal day-to-day life of animals is too vegetable an existence to hold for long the interest of lively human beings. At first we are fascinated by their strangeness, by the way they move and eat and sleep and pass their time. But when the strangeness becomes familiar, the eating and sleeping and passing of time are very dull amusements indeed compared with all the other things that enterprising small boys might be doing. John has just made himself a potter's wheel from the turn-table of an old gramophone. He winds it up and round it goes, and though it tends to fling everything into far corners of the room, he has already made a proud row of small wax vases for Peter to fill with acorns. Does he really think he will want to leave such ingenious delights to clean out a cage of canaries?

It is only in the crises of their lives that pets seem to become interesting again: interesting and moving, for clearly we must first be interested before we can be moved. For months past the healthy pet has been no more than a tiresome animal to be looked after in the evenings when the children had planned to do something else. But a sick pet is a very different matter. A sick pet is an actor in a rich drama where they too have a part. It is not merely an ailing animal but a suffering fellow-creature. Its owners are changed at once from detached observers of its animal life to lovingly involved companions of its trouble. The sick pet has become their brother.

Not that this anthropomorphic rôle suits the poor ill creature. John will hold it firmly in a hot hand and stroke it lovingly but energetically as if it were a sick child. And this must be insufferable torture to all its wild animal instincts. Of course he means well, but that can scarcely be expected to count with the poor wretched pets. For them there is no worse fate than to become the property of friendly small boys who seek extra companions to play with.

Though John has his own detachment about any animals which are fortunate enough not to qualify as pets. "I think it's mean of you to catch the mice," he used to tell me on the farm. "Mice don't eat much. We could easily spare that much food." And I remembered dear Uncle Toby who never killed flies but put them gently out of the window, because the world was wide enough, he said, to hold both him and the flies as well.

But very few people are kind to flies; and even rats, though they are small furry mammals, have not many protectors. The animals we are humane about are a very exclusive family. As for John, he would soon find that it is very difficult indeed to feel for an alligator *as* an alligator. And as a pet to play with it would clearly have most serious drawbacks. Nor can I give up the downstairs wash-basin for the preliminary week or two until the poor creature falls ill enough to qualify as a fellow human being.

All the same I can see that I shall have to do something about the problem of pets, for certainly John will not be put off for long by my piecemeal objections. Change the subject as I may, he will always find some way of bringing it back to a nice hardy canary. I am only surprised that he did not send back his ten shillings for our visitor to buy one there and then, and I suppose if we must share our house with some other animal a canary is as little trouble as any. Though I realize it will have to be two canaryz, for Peter is sure to insist on one as well, when John has once broken through my resistance. It is not that Peter has any particular liking for pets. His reaction to animals is a kindly interest rather than affection, and without John he would be quite content with his Natural History Museum. It is housed (very humbly for all its fine name) on a shelf in his bedroom cupboard, growing dustier every week as the months pass, a messy collection of small skeletons and skulls of birds, of coloured feathers and pressed flowers and odd sticks and stones with careful labels. "Skratch on a stone by a badger's claw." "Damage done to bark of tree by a ~~squiril squirril sqirel~~ squir-rel." I think he must have asked in the end. He is a very erratic speller.

As a housewife I am delighted if museums will take the place of pets. Certainly the shelf is most depressingly dusty, but I have only to keep the cupboard door shut and not look inside. How-

· 73 ·

ever if John has a real live canary, then Peter will want one too.
Of course he will. Anyone would.

But for a week at least John has said nothing about pet-keeping, and I wonder whether he has given up hope of persuading
me or is only considering something even more ambitious, like
an elephant in the yard or a sea-lion in the bath. For I always
mistrust John when he says nothing.

To-night he is sitting at the table in most suspicious idleness,
for when small boys sit most idle they are generally most busy
with plans. Especially John is busy, for John is a great maker of
plans. For the last ten minutes he has sat and watched me preparing supper, standing at the stove stirring two pans at once to save
time. He has been looking at me without seeing, but now rouses
himself from abstraction, and I wait for him to begin some conversation which he will bring round inevitably to things like baby
camels or small-size zebras. For conversation with John lately is
like playing with a ball on sloping ground: no matter where we
start, we always finish up at the same place, at the bottom. But if
zebras are what he has been considering he must feel that this is
no time to approach me, stirring two pans at once. "Mrs. Somebody would never do that, would she? Mrs. Somebody's a lady
you know."

So he informs me in a considering, critical way, as if he would
prefer me a little less homely. "Yes she is," I agree. "But what's
a lady?" I ask hopefully, for the children never seem suspicious
of this kind of illogical answer, perhaps because they are too occupied with getting into words their vague idea of just what it is
they do mean. Though John's ideas are seldom vague. "Well,
ladies wear party clothes all the time and put lots of black round
their eyes, and they're very particular about everything—like
not sitting on chairs with crumbs on the seat. And if they want
their handbag they never fetch it themselves but always send
someone else. And they always have baths full right up to their

· 74 ·

necks and as much bath salts in as ever they want—piles and *piles* of bath salts. Pink.''

I do see that this is most alarmingly accurate observation of Mrs. Somebody, though I can only guess about the baths, as I suppose John must have done too, elaborating with almost poetic suitability. But what seemed to me at John's age the distinguishing mark of superior beings was that they always had their names on all their possessions. It was as if the things themselves had some magical value simply by belonging to these wonderful creatures. There were name-tapes on all their clothes (even their old school socks with darns in the toes), name-plates on their books, initials on their luggage, their sheets, even their handkerchiefs—everything. It seemed to me very strange and wonderful, as if they owned such a wealth of possessions that they could not possibly remember them all. Whereas I had so very few socks that I recognized them individually as my own, name or no name. My books were closely-treasured and intimate companions; I knew every smudge on every cover, every dark line along the edges of the closed leaves where they opened at my favourite pages from long habit. And if our family luggage got lost on journeys, it was not because there were no initials on the suitcases but because my father was quite astonishingly absent-minded.

Even now, though I have sewn dozens and dozens of name-tapes on school socks and shirts and gym-trunks, on caps and ties and football jerseys—even now it still seems to me very grand to have one's humblest clothes labelled, like the kings whose very nail-parings were treasured as precious.

Certainly when I was a child these name-taped people seemed to me a different race of beings. It was not that they were cleverer, for I could see that they were not. It was not because their clothes or houses or motor-cars were different, for that was only a difference of degree, as some children had finer toys than others, but still they were all only toys to play with in the same way as I played with mine—these people were not different in degree, but different in kind. Their values were different, the things they cared about and thought important, even the way they arranged their daily lives. Meals, for instance, were not for them, as they were for me, simply a time for eating food because they were hungry. Meals to them were essentials important in themselves, a mystical pattern of fixed hours into which the day's other activities must be made to fit whether one liked it or not. And they *did* like it, that was what astonished me. They seemed not to mind, even on holiday, that the delightful things they were doing should be interrupted, whether or not they were hungry, by a fixed hour round a table. They were never free, even on holiday. They never woke up suddenly in the early morning and stuffed their pockets with biscuits and apples and slipped out of the house into the whole long glorious day ahead, as free as the clouds sailing over the enormous sky. Not at all. They went a little walk to the village or down to the beach or along the cliff-tops—"But not too far remember, because of being back in time for lunch."

And these meal-time prisoners were prisoners from choice. They arranged their day like this on purpose. Nor was it because they were greedy, nor the food very good, but simply because they liked the routine. It was strange, I felt, beyond my power of understanding (it still is); these were the customs of a different species.

Another thing too, about these well-regulated people, which set them wonderfully apart as a different race from myself, was that they always knew what their lives were going to be like; they seemed to my innocence to be in complete control of their own fate. It was not only the grown-ups who planned their affairs so confidently, who were thinking of moving south, or wondering Should they retire to the town or the country? or considering the advantages of this new post or that. The children too, shared this god-like knowledge of their own future. They were going in for Law, or the Civil Service, or taking Father's place in the family business when he retired.

How they could possibly feel their lives so clear-cut and settled I never could imagine, for quite certainly mine was not. If I belonged to any class at all it was the class of English eccentrics, and there is nothing in the least settled about the future of its children except that it is completely unpredictable. I might finish as queen or beggar-maid, die famous or forgotten, but certainly my life twenty years ahead was as remote and unimaginable as the far side of the moon. There were no plans, no probabilities, no ways of guessing even, which were not as magical as the crystal-gazer's glass. I was swimming by myself, at large in a strange sea which these people crossed in efficient boats to known destinations. In my open-sea swimming I could hear the sirens singing, as they never could through the steady reliable noise of their engines; I caught sideways glimpses of enchanged islands which they never knew existed as they gazed so confidently ahead. I might find high adventure or become a great artist or marry a duke as my great-aunt did. But even as a child I also knew very well that I might drown, that in this perilous sea I had no boat to save me, but must make my own raft to cling to as best I could. And because I grew up in a northern industrial city in the dreadful days of unemployment between the wars, my childish plans were not idle fancies but clear-eyed encounters with possible disaster. It was not that I was likely to be cast out destitute into the wide world like the youngest brother in the fairy tales; but children are more sensitive to atmosphere than logic, and the atmosphere of the city where I lived was a sense of hopeless destitution, with every week more men turned away from work to drag out their unwanted days in wretched idleness, standing in sullen groups at street corners.

Against this sense of disaster in the community my own home was not a close enough protection (no doubt because there were

no initials on the luggage), so that I learned then a consciousness
of the deep drowning sea which I think I shall never lose. And in
self-defence against possible destitution I must have plans; must
decide beforehand exactly what I could do if the worst happened.
In cold unchildlike disillusion I considered what work there was
which I could rely on finding if I had to earn my own living in
poverty—unskilled work clearly, since I was trained for nothing;
work so unpleasant and so badly paid that no-one else wanted it.
There was scrubbing floors, I supposed. But that was too dreadful I felt, being a clean and fastidious child. Nor could I bear to
consider the greasy water and scraps of food of washing dishes
in a restaurant. What I could do, I decided at last, if I really had
to, was work in a laundry. Certainly I shuddered at the thought
of sorting out the dirty clothes of strangers, and that, I supposed,
was the bottom where one started. But since I was quick and
neat with my hands I thought I could soon progress to ironing
shirts, a clean and tolerable way of earning some sort of living
compared with the other possibilities I had looked at from the
bottom of disaster. It was not that I ever intended to work in a
laundry. Quite certainly not. But it is a comfort always to have
considered the worst that can happen, to have faced the haunting
half-recognized ghosts of background anxiety and come to terms
with them.

But certainly I had no intention of ironing shirts, nor of marrying a duke like my great-aunt either for that matter, though
admittedly that seemed a more romantic story in those days. She
was a beautiful actress, and he had to give up his claim to the
throne when he fell in love and married her. All very suitable
I thought, and quite like the fairy tales. But I looked them up
once in the duke's copious memoirs, and the story is only dull
and domestic. To start with he was a cousin of Queen Victoria,
and that is scarcely a romantic beginning for anyone. And although she was beautiful and an actress at Drury Lane, she too
was as virtuous and respectable as any wife could well be. It was

all very disappointing. For if dukes marry actresses in the nineteenth century, we can surely expect it to be gay—rousing parties with dancing on the table and toasts drunk in champagne from the lady's satin slippers.

But not at all—they were a most sedate couple who lived in Charles Street, Mayfair, and their married life was fifty years or so of domesticity so irreproachable that in the end they won even his cousin Victoria's grudging approval. No-one could help feeling cheated that they lapsed so badly from the established tradition of dukes and chorus girls. Yet for all her dullness she seems to have been a dear, my great-aunt Louisa (or perhaps my great-great-aunt—I have forgotten). "Good and kind and affectionate and true and generous-hearted." So her sorrowing husband wrote of her when she died in old age. It is a tribute which speaks more warmly from the heart than most Victorian epitaphs.

However, neither dukes nor laundries had any part in my real plans, which were very different. The whole world lay open before me, and as for the difficulties—they were only there to be jumped over. With my odd background there was no question of doing what was expected of me, for nothing, so far as I can remember, ever *was* expected. Nothing except that I should go out and do what I wanted.

As to what I did want, that was much more difficult to plan for than the laundry. For a time of course, there was the stable-girl-kennel-maid stage which most girls seem to go through, but once recovered from dogs and horses I was quite clear about what I wanted to do. My single simple desire was to meet superior beings and to admire them.

Somewhere, I was convinced, there was a community of brilliant people—wise, beautiful, witty, elegant, gifted, sophisticated, friendly, intelligent people. Such paragons they were in my imagination that even now I marvel only to remember them. They were people who painted pictures, talked like gods, wrote poetry, composed music, did everything desirable: heavenly creatures in fact, who shone serenely in my mind with the light that never was on land or sea or anywhere at all. They lived together somewhere I thought (for I was wonderfully ignorant) in a society of all the wits and graces, exchanging ideas, encouraging each other's work, linked by love and friendship in what seemed to me the ideal life.

Ah well—I kept good company in my day-dreams, though I never knew it. There may even have been halcyon times in human history which might have qualified, though I doubt it. I doubt whether even the golden age of Plato and Socrates would quite have done by my standards: not elegant enough I should imagine. Quite certainly it was not a world I knew at home or at school, for although I admired some of my teachers well enough, they were only the faintest shadows of what I hoped to find out in the unknown world beyond the barrier of factory chimneys which fenced me in. It was not that I wanted to shine myself. I think I never saw myself in any rôle at all except as unseen and anonymous admirer. I simply wanted to watch and marvel in an unqualified outpouring of love and worship.

When I was eighteen I took myself off to London and the University. At last, I thought. At last. Now I shall meet them. Now I shall know. And my eyes dazzled with the brilliance of the world that lay ahead. For I was a romantic young woman, very backward no doubt, and at eighteen I was scarcely more reasonable in my day-dreaming than I was as a child. So that the University was one of the great bewildering disappointments, the profound sorrows which take us years to get used to and change our whole lives: one of the ruthless disillusions which destroy our dreams and turn us into adults.

For here was my dreamed-of community: and here they were —lecturers who were my schoolmasters and mistresses only grown older and more distinguished, and my companions a lot of ex-schoolboys and -schoolgirls as awkward as myself.

The First Three Years Transplanted

It has left me with an untried gift for hero-worship which I have never had a proper chance to use. I dare say now I never shall. And should I really enjoy it I wonder, if I got the chance? It seems an unrewarding pastime for both sides—me endlessly admiring, they endlessly admired. I cannot feel that it would be good for either of us in the end. And since, whether we like it or no, human beings are not conveniently divided into Paragons and Others, there is no choice but to accept the haphazard and only piecemeal excellencies of our fellows. But for years I grieved over the short-comings, seeking always perfection. For I grew up very slowly with my private dreams, far more slowly than Peter and John who will clearly be tolerant adults at an age when I was still a romantic adolescent.

Already they have changed beyond knowing from the naïve anxious children who were plunged into London nearly three years ago. They are at their ease now, gay again and playful, and although the games they play are still the old favourites they have played for years past, there is a new literary flavour which comes no doubt from the large numbers of story-books they bring home from the library now that they read quickly and easily enough to devour books for themselves. They still, when they are alone together, play the same childish games with their old toy trains on the floor: long sagas of locomotive life which meander on through the weeks with adventures added at random from any book they happen to be reading. There are engines who love or hate each other, are friends or enemies. There are families of engines, gangs of engines, engines who are heroes or villains, and who all have the most complicated and violent adventures. And all of them have this in common—they are all, without exception, engines who do a great deal of talking.

As for the characters, these have not changed much since the old pre-library days. The heroes and villains are still simple black and white as they always so comfortably are in saga morality. There are big engines who may be either bad bullies or good protectors, little engines who are sometimes quite astonishingly brave heroes but are most of them timorous creatures, frightened of dark tunnels, nervous of buffers, alarmed by the big ones letting off steam too close beside them.

The general pattern of the stories is much the same as it always was, but nowadays the adventures are more sophisticated, and the running commentary supplied by John and Peter alternatively is in a fine new literary style.

"The Little Engine limped home at last as darkness fell, tired and frightened and unhappy." I wonder how an engine limps? But no doubt it is a quotation from some tale of horses in the Wild West.

"He sat down suddenly" (the children do not seem to be troubled by my too-literal imagination, which tips the engine suddenly back onto its tender with its front wheels spinning helplessly in the air). "He gave a great sigh," and such a gust follows that the bedroom curtains stir in the breeze.

All *oratio recta* is delivered with enormous gusto: frightful screams of "Help! Help! The Dragon!" followed by "said the Little Engine" in a quiet nonchalant voice. "Save my Sunday whiskers!" This is John who can hardly speak for laughing. But whether he is giggling at the thought of an engine with whiskers, or whether he thinks it is a quotation from *Alice in Wonderland*, I have no idea. Certainly he thinks *Alice* is the funniest book in the world, and always chuckles even to remember.

"Spy. Traitor. Imposter." The insults are spat out with venom and conviction. " 'I'll get the truth out of you,' he roared, then laughed quietly, 'Ha ha ha.' " It is the true diabolic laugh of blackest melodrama. "Then they went along the lines, and as it grew dark they came to a tunnel and the tunnel was full of satellites. Some of them hung down from the ceiling and some stood up on the floor." This is John taking his turn with the story, and telling it in the portentous tone which means that something dreadful is going to happen at any moment. But he interrupts himself to explain to Peter in his normal cheerful voice about the stalagmites and stalactites. "I think they have two separate names really, but I can't remember which are which." Well neither can any of us, and it is very convenient to have a comprehensive word.

But what happened in this geologically obstructed tunnel I never found out, for the general atmosphere of gloom was suddenly broken by the voice of an engine I am particularly fond of. It is a very effeminate engine, a dandy of a locomotive, and quite exquisitely affected. It talks in the most languishing of drawls, and says things like "My *dear*. You can't im*agine*." It is easily my favourite character of them all, and I am disappointed always if it does not appear when I stop and eavesdrop at the bedroom door on my way downstairs. But it appears far too seldom, no doubt because the children cannot think of things that such a sophisticated creature would be likely to say.

Trains, I dare say, is a game which will go on for years longer yet, though the actual engines now lack wheels and funnels and paint and almost everything else which distinguishes them as engines. But another favourite game which has changed even more since we came to town is Cat and Mouse. It is a simple and rather improving game invented long ago by William, who produces new games as off-shoots of our ordinary life in a most satisfactory way. For some reason Cat and Mouse was always played after Sunday lunch. We were the cats and the children were the mice. We chased them, caught them, imprisoned them on our knees, asked them questions and tortured them till we got the right answer. The tortures were tickling, squeezing, turning the mice upside down, and any other form of delicious romping which we felt strong enough to go in for immediately after Sunday lunch.

It was a game which very quickly changed its nature, since the cats were always too torpid to do much chasing and the mice were so very eager to be caught. Sitting Cat and Running Mouse was a half-way stage where we cats sat unsportingly on our chairs and the mice hopped about at arm's length, closer and closer until we grabbed them. After a time they gave up any pretence of being caught, and sat firmly on our knees as soon as we swallowed down the last spoonful of pudding. For it is odd how much children like being questioned, such dull questions too, like what is the capital of Canada? and where is Timbuctoo? and tell me three flowers beginning with R, and how do you spell rhinoceros? (Though that is a question I should never ask, for I should never know whether their answer was right or wrong, and I should not like them to know that even at my great age my spelling is only slightly better than Peter's.)

The game has now reached what must surely be its dying stage, for since we protest that these large boys are *far* too heavy to sit on our knees any longer, they bring up chairs and sit beside us. And it is they who torture us now instead of the other way round. They prod us and pat us and gently shake us, being careful to keep a very exact balance between the stimulus just lively enough to produce questions, but yet not annoying enough to make us break off the game in irritation.

Sometimes, since we are now so clearly the victims, they ask us questions instead, but this is a variation of the game which we seldom encourage, for the questions of children have always been a notorious hazard for parents, and Peter's questions are mostly unanswerable, problems far too important to wait for games of Cat and Mouse. "How can people live in hot and cold countries if elephants and polar bears can't?" he will greet me on the doorstep arriving home from school. Or shouting above the roar and clatter on top of the bus, "Why don't brothers marry sisters like cows do?"

And once at a fancy-dress party, disguised as the inevitable pirate chief, he suddenly stopped and looked up at me. "Which is most important," he wanted to know, "people's politics or their religions?"

He stood quite still in the middle of the room, abstracted, withdrawn, utterly unconscious of the hubbub all about him, the flying streamers and tumbling children and the pelting with balloons.

"Dardy. Tell me. Which matters most?" And he looked at me entreatingly with one blue eye, since the other was covered with a black pirate's patch. And because he needed so much to know the answer, the false moustaches drooped despairingly each side of his serious mouth. And his face changed, as I have often seen it change, so that it was no longer a child's face, but the face of an adult playing patiently at being a child, playing without understanding what the game was for, but only to please the grownups because it was expected.

And the pirate's red scarf and the gold ear-rings and the Wellington boots were suddenly ridiculous. The clothes were ridiculous, not the child, for Peter has a curious adult dignity always. He is not easily a child. Without John I think he would never romp or play, or laugh for sheer nonsense. Left to himself he is neither gay nor mischievous. Sometimes it is as if he suffered his inevitable childhood as he would suffer an illness, quietly and sadly, with a strange resigned patience that it should take so long to grow to the full mental stature which he seems unconsciously to await. It is as if he were blind yet somehow knew that sight existed, and knew too that if he waits and is patient, he too will be able in time to see the world which he now only senses all about him. It does not suit him being a child. He is lucky to have John so happily for brother. For left alone he is seldom lighthearted, but serious always.

"Do you know what H.M.S. means?" he asked John one Sunday lunch of Cat and Mouse. But John is bored with information. This is the kind of thing he found out long ago, and the game is getting far too solemn for his idea of fun.

"H.M.S. means His Majesty's Socks," he tells his brother, trying not to giggle just in case Peter should be simple enough to believe him. "And do you want to know what a criminal is? A criminal's a man in stolen socks who sells oranges. And a war criminal's someone who's swallowed a bottle with a frog inside."

Peter is slow always to suspect that he is being made fun of, but even for Peter these flights of fancy are too airy to follow. He glares at his brother, making up his mind to attack him for revenge, but John was ready for flight before Peter even grew suspicious, was off his chair some time ago and hovering near the door. Now he is through and away before Peter can catch him, clattering down the hall, thumping upstairs, breathless already with laughing. And for us there is the great advantage that the ultimate pounding and scuffling and giggling are far enough off to be out of hearing, and we are left in peace and quiet to enjoy our coffee.

If adults wish to talk to children they should always be wary. For though children are blindly insensitive to the feelings of other people, about their own feelings no-one could possibly be more touchy. It is not that we are likely to be unkind, not so much that we shall hurt them as that we shall offend them. What they resent and watch for with never-resting suspicion is that we may make fun of them. We may mock and they will not know why. I think there are few things more upsetting for an intelligent child than to be laughed at without understanding the joke. Nor is it fair to expect them to laugh at themselves; that presupposes a degree of detachment unlikely in the very young. About themselves they are intensely serious, and so must we be if we want them to talk to us. We must converse quite simply as if they were sensible adults, and unless they intend to surprise us we must never be surprised at anything they say. If we are, they will at once take fright and say not another word for fear of seeming ridiculous. And sometimes, if we are patient, there are unexpected treasures.

"There aren't any misers nowadays, are there?" John wanted to know one night in bed when I went in to turn off the light.

The First Three Years Transplanted

"I don't quite know what a miser is," I lied hopefully, for I have learned to hedge, realizing long ago what a mistake it is to correct without thinking the peculiar ideas of children.

"Well, a miser's someone who makes a lot of money, but he doesn't notice it because he works so hard. Then one day he gets rheumatism or something and he can't work any more, and then he finds he's got all this lot of money. But he doesn't want people to know, so he wears ragged clothes and puts ragged curtains up at the windows so that everyone thinks he's poor. But he's only artificial poor you see, really, and that's a miser."

"Artificial" is their word of the moment, for like all children —like adults too for that matter—Peter and John will take a sudden liking for some new word and use it for a time at every sentence end. While it is in fashion it seems to express with perfect precision almost everything they want to say, as our new words always do, and we wonder how we ever managed without them. "Artificial" they find quite unexpectedly useful, widening its range to include all kinds of subtle meanings for which they had no word till now.

"That's the one with the artificial belt," they say of an old family raincoat which has lost its belt and uses a luggage strap instead. Or of a child in the street, screaming to attract attention, "He's not hurt you know. He's crying on purpose. That's only artificial crying. If you smacked him he'd stop." For like all children they are clear-sighted and ruthless observers of their own kind. They themselves have what they shrewdly call their artificial quarrels, explosions of anonymous irritation quite without personal malice. And there was the history lesson which I overheard the other day. "Yes. I *know* the king was his father," Peter explained to John in the self-satisfied voice of the well-informed who explain to the ignorant. "But *he* couldn't be king because of his mother. He was only the king's artificial son."

Certainly it has often been put less delicately, and they know quite well what they mean, for I asked them and they told me with great clarity. There seem to be unexpected educational advantages in growing up with the down-to-earth sex of the farm-yard.

But Cat and Mouse and Definitions are far too much like the clever games with pencil and paper that intellectuals used to play at parties. They are not what I mean by playing, and not what John means either, though he is always ready to join in. Much more John's idea of fun is the game they call Roof Riding, a very simple game for me, and one I would always play in the country, though I think they must really give it up in the town. I open the sunshine roof of the car, and they take it in turns to stand on the seat and ride with their head and shoulders out of the top. Roof Riding is as simple as that, but when they were little the children found it quite deliriously exciting. Did they feel they were flying I wonder, as we do in dreams? or imagine themselves on the prow of a ship or the front of an engine? Whatever it was, they never told me, only grew so attached to their game that even now they give it up reluctantly, and in the first excitement of early spring they cast the dignity of age aside at the call of such headlong delight.

It is not a pleasure only for the spring of course, but certainly it does not do for frozen winter, and the first roof-riding of the year is always a sudden wild exhilaration of the first soft weather, a sudden impatience of our earth-bound state.

Whoever thinks of it first has first turn, and it is generally John. He takes off his shoes (I insist), climbs on the seat, clutches the edge of the roof and surveys the world outside, his face brilliant with excitement.

"Go on! Go on!" He shakes the car with impatience for me to start, and straddles his legs more firmly as we go round the first corner, his hair already streaming in the wind like water. At first there is no need to drive fast, for clearly a head through a roof gets a quite different idea of speed from a head enclosed in a car. We are travelling as sedately-slow as an invalid out for a first ride, but for John we must be flashing through the streets like a racing-car, for I can see his knuckles white where he grasps the roof, his toes gripping the edge of the seat through his socks, and all his body taut with exhilaration. It is as if he felt at any moment he might soar through the roof like a rocket and leave us far below.

We drive on steadily and Peter begins to grow bored, to fidget with impatience for his turn.

"We're only going at twenty miles an hour and John thinks that's *fast*," he says with scorn, leaning over from the back seat to read the speedometer.

"I know," I answer, for the passengers amuse themselves by conspiring against the roof rider. "But John thinks it's sixty at least, so I don't need to go any faster." Peter grins maliciously, for it is one of the games of the people sitting tamely inside that we can say whatever we like and the outside head can hear nothing at all but the glorious rush of the wind in his ears. So we enliven our boredom by making outrageous statements about our deaf companion.

"John's a silly ass," says Peter. "He's sillier than anyone in the whole world. He's so silly he doesn't even care when I say so." Even to Peter this sounds very mild, but he has no real gift for invective. When they were young, as they would say, it used to be very simple. "John's got a purple nose." "Peter's got green hair." Quite simple statements were the most uproarious of jokes. But now they have grown so very old they feel the need of real invective, and that is a gift granted only to a few, being a kind of poetry. Peter and I are no Falstaffs or Macbeths. "If you say yes before I count ten I'll give you anything in the world you like. So will Dardy," Peter adds as an afterthought. He counts ten with relish, lingering over the unheard numbers, ready to gabble them off in a rush if John shows signs of coming in before the end. But I can feel that he will not be patient much longer.

John crouches down and joins us inside for a moment, a creature from another element, his hair dragged back like a hurricane, his eyes streaming with tears he cannot stop to wipe away. "How fast are we going?" He sees the pointer at 25 and is crestfallen. "Is that all? Can't we go faster? Go on. You drive and I'll tell you when it's too fast." He takes up his stand again like a figure-head breasting the running sea of air.

"Go on. Faster. Faster, *faster*, FASTER." People in cars passing the other way smile at him and wave, and he waves back frantically.

"Go on. As fast as ever you can. It's *wonderful*." We can just hear his words, torn snatches in the wind which plasters his shirt flat against his chest and balloons it in a flapping sail behind. But it really is Peter's turn now, and we slow down to a stop for the changeover. John gives up his place reluctantly, but Peter pushes him impatiently out of the way and scrambles to his feet, quick and tense, clutching the edge of the roof with both hands. He talks less than John, never waves to passing cars, but stands rigid, a tranced figure, drugged with the violence of speed, blind and deaf and delighted. In the end he comes in of his own accord and sinks down in the seat with a great sigh of satisfaction.

But they really are too old now for these childish excitements we brought to town with us from the country. They must give them up if for no other reason than that they have grown too tall and project too absurdly far through the roof, no longer their head and shoulders only, but everything above the waist. They must find other, discreter amusements than this driving round the streets with everyone turning to look as we go by. But what will they find to take its place I wonder? For as we grow older our reliable pleasures are harder to come by, not simpler as children suppose, seeing us omnipotent with all the world to choose from. The pleasures of middle-age are more subtle and complicated than anything that children imagine, are no longer separate parcelled-up delights which we can enjoy when we please, like toys in the cupboard waiting to be played with. The pleasures of adult people must be rooted in their ordinary life to be satisfying, are occasions of everyday living enhanced and made significant, not separate amusements added from outside. It is as if our lives were a kind of architecture, which is not decorated by choosing trimmings and sticking them on the finished edifice, but by conceiving units of the actual building as decoration—windows and entrances and roofs. In the finest of all, the entire structure becomes a perfectly satisfying whole, but that is more than ordinary mortals can hope for in their lives. Most of us can only cultivate our existence in patches here and there, meeting our friends, planting our gardens, sharing in the life of the town. But nowhere any Roof Riding. Nowhere anything as simple and self-contained. For adults alas, there are no reliable slot-machines where we can put in our pennies and pull out a slab of pleasure at the other end like chocolate.

These are the things which Peter will soon understand, but John I think will only learn later on, sadly, as adult disillusion. Though it is possible that John may never have to learn them, that his active gift for enjoying the simplest occasions will last all his life.

But both of them, by my age, will have found out for themselves which are the things that matter when they look back; will remember as I do the evenings with friends—with one friend, or two or three, or a party perhaps in winter, with warm lights and the darkness cold outside, or on some perfect summer evening half a dozen companions come together to eat and talk in company. For there are summer evenings sitting with friends which we remember always. When the day has ebbed at last, a day too noisy and dusty and hot, too full of strangers and traffic and rushing from one crowded place to another. But now we sit peacefully together, and the evening has come to rest at last in the quiet room, like a marble settling gently into the hollow of a bowl.

We have eaten together and chattered round the dinner table, laughing and lively and saying quick things to amuse our neighbours. But the laughing and chattering belonged to the day behind us, they were part of the meeting and the journey to come together across the town. Now the meal is over, and we are back in this quiet room looking over the garden, and we too are quiet at last.

We all know each other. There is no need to talk until we wish to. We can choose our chair for the evening, and settle down in silence beside the wide windows opening onto the steep green slope of this Hampstead lawn. It is warm and summer. The high trees outside are swaying and heaving in the soft wind, and half-heard beyond their leafy murmuring is another steadier murmur, a low and far-off hum which is all that reaches us in this peaceful house of the teeming noisy life of London.

We are settled now, scattered in low chairs about the room, lolling at our ease. The sideways sunlight of late evening is still bright on the wall against the window, glowing on the paint of pictures and the coloured covers of books. But already the air is mysterious with the oncoming dark, and in the corners dusk is already waiting to flow out into the room and blur the spaces between us.

At first the talk is desultory. A single remark and an answer, or now a little flow of conversation, then laughter and a settling down again more comfortably in chairs. It is as if we were all waking slowly from some trance of silence which separated this quiet evening from the rest of our bustling day; and when we wake we shall no longer be separate fragmentary units who have hurried from the affairs of our scattered lives to meet each other for dinner; we shall be transformed to a harmonious group of friends, united and contained in this shadowy bowl of the evening, as random colours are composed into a picture by combining them on a canvas.

The sun has moved now from the wall against the window. Outside in the garden the long shadow of the lime-tree slants further across the lawn, and on the terrace the sunlight no longer reaches even the highest branches of the bush of ceanothus beside the window. In the shadow of the wall the blue flowers glow now with a strangely luminous quality, paler than they were in the daytime, as blue flowers are always paler at night and red flowers darker.

But the voices are beginning now, and I must rouse from my trance as the others are rousing from theirs. Inside the room there is a feeling of people waking up for the evening; first one figure, then another, sit up a little in their chairs, rearrange their elbows more alertly on the chair-arms, recross their legs, fidget a little, lean forward—all the small restless signs of people who are going to talk. Even without seeing their faces we can feel from the depths of the chair the expectancy which means they are waiting for a pause in the flow of voices because there is something they want to say. One of the men asks another what he thinks of a new book a friend has written. A woman says something to her neighbour and they both laugh. But I only half hear what they are saying, for I am fascinated, not by their words but by the sound of their voices, by the sound of man the animal making his own particular noise. For this easy talk is one of the most personal of man's many noises: not commands nor information nor any expression of feeling or emotion, but quiet friendly talk with his fellows, talk for pleasure and at ease, as intimate as the sub-song of a bird twittering to itself on a branch in the winter sunshine. This is how minds converse together: language as man's self-made means of communication.

I shut my eyes to listen, though there is no need to in this shadowy room. And as always when we listen to the voices not the words, what we are conscious of is the cadences of talking, the pitch and rhythm so personal to each of us that we can tell who is speaking, simply by the rise and fall of sound through the wall from one room to another, without recognizing either the words or even the note of the actual voices. Nor is it only between individual people that the cadences vary. Different languages too have different rhythms, unmistakable even at a distance too great to hear any separate words. The French mouth and savour their language as if it were food, the Italians mould the phrases with their voice like sculptors, and Americans handle their language so roughly that it is as if they insulted it. Until we get used to Americans talking their mildest remarks sound quite disconcertingly like swearing.

And English? I listen to the voices. There are several people talking at once now, in a contrapuntal pattern of individual rhythms, but still all with enough family likeness to blend easily together. I listen, but it is hard to tell with one's own language. There are strong beats with running mumbled passages between, more light and shade perhaps than in languages more clearly spoken. But no. It is all too relaxed and easy to be impressive. These patterns of single accents against a background of slurred syllables have a light informal effect. I listen again, sitting back deep in my chair, hoping that no-one will draw me into the talk.

It is an oddly secret-sounding language, as if we spoke always in asides to each other and not to a public audience. But someone is saying that he will fit a clock to his gramophone so that every morning, instead of a dreary alarm bell, it will wake him triumphantly to Purcell's "Trumpet Voluntary." And everyone joins in and chooses his own morning record, and no-one listens to anyone else, for the choosing of favourites is a private pleasure and needs no audience.

The last sun has faded now even from the highest leaves of the lime-tree, and the twilight is gathering in the garden, held by the steep surrounding walls like dark water in a pool. The room grows dim and shadowy, but no-one will destroy this enchanted dusk by turning on the lamps. A man leans forward to emphasize the point of what he is saying, emerging for a moment from the darkness of his chair. There is a sudden flare of argument, laughter, a woman's fair head moving quickly, half-seen and pale in the shadow. In the growing dark we are mysteriously remote from each other, linked only by our disembodied voices; as if the carpet were a lake and we floated in our chairs like boats, each one separate but close together, calm upon still water.

I listen now to what they are saying—about some odd event in the morning paper, about the astonishing beauty of the new wife of someone we all know well, about a village in the Appennines with wonderful unknown frescoes in the church.

And I think how the talk of men and women is quite different —except that of course it is absurd to talk of men and women as if we were different species, whereas our sex is an arbitrary accident added to people all much alike, or rather to people not at all alike but differing from each other in ways which have nothing to do with sex. But since there are masculine qualities and feminine qualities, even though these are not shared out logically between men and women as we might expect—but since there are differences of conception however they may apply to actual individuals, masculine talk is not the same as feminine talk. Men make statements, present facts; they argue and discuss. Women create atmosphere; explore not facts but personalities; they control the relationships between the speakers. Masculine talk alone is bleak and unsubtle and inharmonious. Feminine talk lacks abstract subjects, has too many implications, too few facts. Good conversation needs both ingredients in the mixture to make a satisfactory whole. And I think to myself that it is probably why homosexual men are often such excellent talkers.

They are arguing now about the French Revolution. But I can never be interested for long in the French Revolution, and I listen instead to the spacing and overlapping of their arguments, to the unemphatic cadences, and the rise and fall of their voices against the sighing background of the trees, coming and going on the wind like a waterfall a long way off.

The French Revolution was this, they say. The French Revolution was that. But a wave of watery sound flows in from the garden, then dies away again through the valley trees like the noise of a distant wave running back down a pebbly shore. And my mind wanders off from what they are saying. I think of Delacroix' energetic pictures of white-breasted young women waving flags on barricades; and how it can never have been in the least like that (not nearly so clean for one thing). And I remember how it was one of the few dates I could remember at school, 1789 like a telephone number specially arranged. Easier really than our favourite 1066. And how odd it is if we think of it, that this one date every English person remembers with amused affection, is the date our country was conquered by a foreign invader. So that it is not true, what Peter said to me scornfully the other day, that the battles they teach you about in history lessons are always the ones our own side wins. And because we think so much faster than we speak, the talkers are still in the middle of their Revolution, the same argument is still going on, the same two speakers are still trying to convince each other of their opposing theories.

The room where we sit is almost dark now, and the peopled chairs are only darker shadows. Beyond the wide windows and the glass doors open onto the terrace, the garden still faintly glimmers; but grey now in the late twilight, green-grey and blue-grey and grey which is almost black in the angle beneath the wall. And because the dim room has lost its identity, the world outside flows in through the doors and windows and fills the space around us. It is not the room we are conscious of now but the garden. We are no longer surrounded by tables and book-shelves but by leaves and flowers. It is grass under our feet now, not carpet. And although the voices are still talking all around me, it is the fainter sounds from outside that I hear most clearly —the surge and rustle of the leafy trees, and across the hillside, far off and faint, the constant murmurous noises of the town.

The First Three Years Transplanted

How cool it is out here in spirit on the lawn, and how infinitely high the sky seems now it is drained of all colour but this remote receding grey. The lime-tree above me heaves and tosses with the full bosomy richness of high summer. There is a star among the lower branches—or is it a street lamp perhaps, newly-lit on the opposite hillside? Is that a copper beech next to the lime-tree? It is hard to tell, only that it is a darker moving shadow among shadows. But somewhere near there is a poplar, for though I cannot see it, the rustle of poplar leaves is unmistakable always, like the myriad pattering of a sudden summer shower.

Even to make out the near-by flowers in the border under the wall I must concentrate. Is that a red peony black against dark leaves? Not roses yet, it is too soon in the summer for roses, or peonies either—but that pale greyish streak against the wall— that surely is a lupin.

It is cold now the light has gone. I shiver a little and clasp my bare arms. "*Frileuse*" the French would call it, a word which exactly captures this summer shiveriness—half cold, and half our pleasure in being cold after the heat of the day. A black cat with white legs passes swiftly along the top of the wall above me, its body gliding with a motion of flowing water uninterrupted by the twinkling of its legs beneath. A bat flitters over and disappears in the darkness between the trees.

I sit completely still in my chair, for if I moved, even so much as a finger, I should be tethered again to my indoor body, no longer free to float. But since I have sat so still for so long I am unaware now of any part of my physical shell. Without looking I cannot tell where my feet are on the carpet, nor my hands on the arms of the chair. I am disembodied. My consciousness passes in and out of the room as simply as the summer air, and the sounds of the garden and the voices in the room rise and fall against each other in alternate waves on my ears, ebbing and flowing.

The friendly voices sound remote now and portentous like voices in dreams, and the ordinary things they say seem strange and mysterious.

"But then we lost them and no-one ever heard of them again."

"You should go to Ireland, they all talk like angels."

"No we never did. The hill was too steep."

Momentary fragments against the gently heaving trees, poignant and lovely beyond anything they say, as poetry is.

And as I listen I realize again how separate we all are for most of our lives, and how difficult it is to reach one another on any level which matters. As if all human beings were separate spinning spheres which could only touch at single surface points. But that to-night is different. To-night we are close to each other as we seldom are, as if to-night the spheres had come together in a pattern, and we were no longer separate units but felt the others near and comprehensible, close around us on every side.

And I feel how these are my friends and I love them; love their familiar remembered voices, and the way they laugh, and their gaiety and warmth and understanding. And I know that for me this evening together will be one of the memories we keep with us always, to guard us from loneliness, and save us perhaps from despair.

But between the voices now there are silences. The evening is almost over. It is late. Far too late. We must go. We must rouse ourselves and say good-night and all go home to bed.

One after another we unfold ourselves reluctantly from chairs. Our host turns on a light and at once the room springs back to consciousness. The ghostly garden has vanished at a touch. Only the nearest branches of the ceanothus catch the brightness from the window, like a bush in a stage set. The enchantment is broken, we are only ordinary people, separate again, stiff from sitting so long, foolishly blinking in the sudden light. And the evening is over, the precarious complicated peace, the exactly accordant perfection of time and place and mood and people.

The First Three Years Transplanted

There are never for any of us many such meetings. We may spend a hundred summer evenings with our friends and none of them like this. For these are not occasions we can create simply by taking thought: by inviting the right people, and giving them wine and food and chairs to sit and talk in. Do what we will the evening may be nothing more than an everyday sociable meeting. The spheres may never move together into a pattern: the kingfisher may not come. And there is nothing we can do but arrange the setting and hope that he may. There is no way of persuading so chancy a bird, and our enticing will only drive him away. Kingfishers do not come, alas, simply because we have put out the fish.

PART TWO

THREE
YEARS OF
GROWING

IT IS THREE YEARS NOW SINCE WE CAME TO
London, not long enough perhaps to count as Londoners yet,
but still enough to feel no longer bewildered. The children go
down the street now, not up, to catch their different morning
bus. It is a milestone in their growing-up, for they have left their
first London school and gone on to the next, changing from one
to the other as unconcernedly as changing chairs across the
hearthrug: a pair of experienced school-goers at their third
school already. From the first day they started they insisted on
making their own way there and back, scorning to be fetched
and carried by a nursery mother, for they are no longer overwhelmed by the panic of the lost if they over-ride the proper bus-
stop and are put down bewildered and alone in some strange part
of the town they never knew existed. Three years ago the next
bus-stop into the unknown was as remote from home as the
mountains of the moon. In those early days they were lost: lost
utterly. They would never find their way back to the world
they knew. The city would swallow them and I should never
know—waiting in vain for them to come back for tea—should
never know what had happened: that the friendly red everyday

bus had changed suddenly to a treacherous monster, carrying them off from their precariously familiar world into the dreadful limbo which waited on all sides to engulf them only one bus-stop further on. Three years ago they lived with panic all about them, reassurance was no more than skin-deep, and beneath the familiar surface unknown horrors waited to break through.

But now Peter stays on the bus beyond his stop to find out whether it takes him any nearer the library, and John arrives cheerfully on the doorstep an hour after his usual time.

"Sorry. Am I frightfully late? Sorry." But he is only polite, not repentant, knowing I never worry. "I was reading my comic on the bus and missed the stop and went *miles* too far. And I couldn't be bothered to walk back the same way, so I went what I thought was a short cut and got lost and *lost* and LOST. But I found a lovely shop in a backstreet that sells all sorts of things like little electric motors and bits of wood to make things and special glue that sticks anything you want. That's why I'm so late—stopping to look in the window. And I'm *starving* hungry."

The children, since they were transplanted young, will grow up to be indigenous Londoners, and even I feel at home now in my city life, and no longer a new-comer conscious of a different background. I am as used now to the nearness of my fellow-creatures as I was on the farm to the cows and hens: I am no more disturbed by their presence. As I knew they would, the noises of the town have run together to a sociable background hum of human companionship. The traffic in the streets and the movements of my neighbours and the voices from the mews behind are no longer separate and significant, but blurred to a pleasant tissue of friendly sound, making a backcloth to my day, like the pattern of the wall-paper in a room where we live. Only the ringing of the telephone bell still keeps its original urgency and significance, for to anyone in a doctor's household the telephone is not a background noise at all, but rather a fire-alarm which summons us imperiously, waking us instantly from sleep or dreaming, demanding so insistently to be answered that even in the street, passing an open window with a telephone ringing beyond, I turn instinctively to answer it, troubled and uneasy that it should be left to ring so long unregarded.

I remember the country now less often than I did, only reminded by changes of weather in our narrow sky. Will there be snow on the hills perhaps? Or the trees wild and tossing in the rising wind? After three years we feel at home, the children and I transplanted, and as for William—William was never a country cousin: he was born of a different race, of those who dwell in cities and belong there by instinct. It is the country he must learn as a strange place, where he must keep to the ways he knows or he will be lost: lost irretrievably with no way at all of finding his way back. For put him in a green field and turn him round twice and he may never, alas, find his way home again. He must keep to the paths he has learned, or if he tries some new way—tires of his old walks and sets off to find what lies over the hill-top— then one of us must always go with him the first few times to bring him safely back again.

It is not that he can find his way any better about a town. In Paris, so he tells me, when he is alone he can only find which way to go by climbing to the top of the Arc de Triomphe and looking. But since where he wants to go is mostly at the other side of the city, it leaves him little time for anything else but the Arc de Triomphe. Even though he lived in Paris once for half a year it made no difference, he says. He is mildly querulous. It is only fortunate that he admires the Champs Elysées so wholeheartedly that he never tires of it, so that whenever I think of William in Paris I think of him walking up and down the Champs Elysées in the sunshine and smiling with pleasure.

In our three years of London there have been other, more tangible changes. For one thing the children have grown enormously and to their great satisfaction. For height is now as important almost as age, and on the bedroom door-post they each have their own side where they mark up their height as they used to in the country on the nursery wall, measuring themselves from time to time when they feel they may have grown. They fling off their shoes and stand in their stocking-feet against the door-post, rigid, long-necked as hens, stretching up to the highest fraction of an inch while I balance a book level on their head, and mark the height and the date on the white paint of the door-post. And all the time the one who is waiting his turn watches suspiciously to see that heels are flat on the floor and no cheating by standing on tip-toe.

No matter how often they measure themselves they always seem to have grown, an ascending ladder of pencil-lines climbing steadily towards the black stripe they have drawn solid and unchanging far above and labelled DARDY. That is my height and their ambition. When once they are as tall as I am, they feel, then they will be men at last and their childhood left safely behind them. But I am tiresomely tall and they still have a wide gap to climb through on their ladder—reassuringly wide still, I notice, for the gap is the symbol of my authority marked up on their very door-post.

But if I am taller, they are certainly solider, squarer-built and sturdy. They are no longer soft and pliable children holding my hand, but hard bony boys now, with large knees and awkward elbows. If we bump into each other it is I who bounce off now, not them; they are heavier than I am at the same level. And like the young of animals which will grow large later on, their feet are enormous and out of all proportion to the rest. In football boots they look so immovably weighted to the ground that I feel if they fell over they would rock upright again with no effort at all, like the little dolls with a weight at the bottom which I played with as a child.

There are other changes too in our household world. John has inherited William's first typewriter as he always hoped he

would, and the sheets of practice typing I find on his desk are as
surprising in their different way as William's used to be.

A VERY NICESTORY

    one day i was walking when suddenly out of thebushes
came a slinking tiger i ran for my life there was

      a growl bihind me i screamed oh mummy help me
   but she was nowhere to be seen i had began to cry

Priestley is a silly ass   HHAA   HHAA
Wilkins is a silly ass   yah   boo sucks

There are other changes. In the long Battle of the Pets John
has won his canaries, and as he expected, they seem to be nice
and hardy. They live in a cage on his bedroom window-sill, scat-
ter seed all over the floor, and sing with deafening persistence
whenever we turn on a tap in the bathroom next door to them.
Very loud singers they are, and not at all, I should think, the
kind of voices which win prizes in bird-singing competitions.
For when they sing they rattle the jars and tins and penknives on
John's dressing-table. As their owner, John is fairly satisfied but
as I foresaw, he finds their caged life much less interesting than he
expected, even though in the spring they behaved very strangely,
and John made immediate plans for covering one wall of his bedroom with cage after cage of young canaries.

"You see. If they laid six eggs, say. And those grew up into
three pairs of canaries and laid three *more* lots of six eggs . . ."
And so on and so on—it is the most encouraging kind of arithmetic. He gave them a nesting bowl with a tiny pot egg to encourage them to lay, and how the egg could have disappeared
one morning we have never any of us been able to imagine. It is
one of the unsolved household mysteries.

"Poor things," said John. "They won't know what to do.
They haven't any mother to show them." No mother indeed! I

am dismayed always at the strange duties expected of me. But John is full of plans.

"Shall we put a marble in instead? Do you think they'd notice it wasn't an egg?" But whether they noticed or not, they laid no eggs, and John has given up canary-breeding and set his heart instead on letting them out in his bedroom so that he can tame them to sit on his finger.

About that I am quite determined. They are not coming out of their cage. If need be I shall deliver a flat No and end all argument. I know very well how much mess loose birds make in bedrooms (even Gilbert White complained of the robins) and besides, if they fly loose they will sooner or later escape. And I simply will not be involved in the tragedy of lost pets. An escaped canary would be just as much one's suffering brother as a sick canary, and I can perfectly well imagine the tears, the gloom over the whole house, the heart-broken visits to police stations, the anxious watchings through windows, the rushing home from school to greet me on the doorstep with "Has it come back? *Has* it come back?" I would much rather say No now than then.

But John is best dealt with by his own kind of warfare. A bludgeoning No will silence him, but he has more respect for victories won by strategy. And luckily—luckily for me, not for her, poor thing—the caretaker last week lost her budgerigar which followed her unnoticed from the kitchen and slipped out and away when she went to open the door for the postman. And now, as John says, stopping in front of me on the staircase halfway up to bed, sighing in sudden sympathy for all lost and lonely creatures, "It must be feeling *dreadfully* sad, poor little thing, all by itself out there in the dark."

His voice trails off mournfully and I can see one corner of his drooping mouth. It is a fate which even John hesitates to risk for his own canaries. Then he turns round to face me on the step above, his eyes level with mine, and he smiles at me in purest mischief.

"But you know, my dear, *I* never *do* open the door for the postman." And he flings his arms round my neck and hugs me, and we laugh so much that we have to sit down on the step together for fear we shall both roll downstairs helplessly laughing.

Peter listens to such arguments but says nothing. He has no concern now with the canaries, one way or the other. For although they were a Christmas present, one each, Peter is not really a keeper of pets, and made his half-share over to John as soon as he reasonably could. If he were not too kind-hearted to admit it even to himself, Peter would really prefer his canary dead. He would like to examine it in detail and at leisure. For even as a small child on the farm his interest in the animals was not John's companionable delight in pets, but an embryo interest in comparative anatomy. He examined dead creatures with a quite unsentimental curiosity, yet very gently, as if he loved and respected them. Skulls in particular interested him. "I like to see how the shapes are all like each other, but different," he once explained to me. "And where the holes are that their ears and eyes and things come in and out of." So birds found dead in the garden were boiled in an old saucepan, regardless of the smell, until their bones came clean. Sheep and rabbit skulls were carried home as treasure from our walks in the fields, and when the Farmer killed a marauding fox, Peter buried it in the dung-heap in the cow-yard, examining it gingerly from time to time to see whether the bones were eaten bare enough to be washed clean and put in his collection.

"Do you remember?" he asked me not long ago, "once on the farm me and John found a dead robin. And we buried it in my garden under that little tiny rose-tree you gave me. Do you remember?"

I can remember no particular burial, for burying dead creatures is always a favourite game of children: birds wrapped in scraps of coloured silk, beetles in nests of cotton-wool in matchbox coffins, and on their graves thimbles of water with bunches of tiny flowers—chickweed and speedwell and little tufts of cow-parsley.

But "Yes," I said, lying. "Yes, I remember." For this was clearly important to Peter, something he wanted to tell me, remembering uneasily from his other life after all these years.

"Well, I didn't really bury it under the rose-tree to be nice to the robin. I buried the robin so that when it decayed it would make my rose-tree grow better." And he smiled with a wry half-rueful detachment from his former self. "And you said how kind I was, and I didn't like to tell you because it made me seem so nasty to the robin."

Dear Peter. He need not worry. I am always on the side of the living rose-tree. But Peter is his own critic, a thoughtful observer of himself as well as others. He struggles to see impartially, to judge by what seem to him fair abstract principles.

"Frailty thy name is Woman"

It was the astonishing title I found in an exercise-book he left on the table one night, an essay he was set to write for home-work. But whatever did the master expect on such a subject, I wonder, from a solemn innocent of ten years old? Yet Peter seems to consider it reasonable enough, or perhaps it is that to children everything adults do has been so unpredictable always, that they have learned to accept the extraordinary without wonder.

"Frailty thy name is Woman"

Peter has written it out in a round copy-book hand which makes it irresistibly ridiculous. But he is quite serious, as he always is, and reading it through I realize that he watches our family life far more closely and shrewdly than I ever suspected.

"I do not think that this is true," he begins. "I do not think that a woman is frail. I think that she should be hard-working in the house while her husband goes and earns the living. In the house I think the woman should have the say about domestic matters, even when the husband is at home. In other words, the amount of work you do, the same amount of Government you get. But the woman should never have a stronger hold on the Government than the man, even if she sometimes works harder. But I think that they should reach agreements over all things and not try to run each other's business."

Well. So that is what we look like to Peter, William and I. On the whole he seems approving, but what alarming detachment. I wonder if I should keep his essay-book and show it later on to his young ladies, as a warning of what he expects in the way of a wife. But how could they tell from so cool an analysis that he loves his home as the snuggest and most delightful of private worlds? How could they know that behind his reserve, Peter, far more than most children, is trusting and affectionate? Perhaps the more vulnerable hearts are seldom worn on sleeves: it scarcely seems a comfortable place for them. For more even than most children, Peter needs affection; needs it as constantly and reliably as an animal needs warmth to live. Without it he grows numb with cold, uneasy and bewildered, not only in his feeling but in his thinking too, his mind as useless and clumsy as agile fingers stiff with frost. He can learn nothing from teachers he does not like. It is not that he is obstinate, but as if his mind were only open and receptive in the steady warmth of reliable affection, as if our minds were plants growing in the climate of our emotions, and unless the climate suits them they cannot thrive.

There are people who are stimulated by the cold, are more alert and active in bracing weather than in languid summer. John for that matter does well enough in a changeable climate, he hardens off like greenhouse flowers set out in the garden, and goes on growing more vigorously at the new temperature. But Peter needs a background of settled warm weather for his unhindered development. The wind and cold oppress him, and destroy the sunny calm he needs if he is ever to grow to his full stature. I think his mind creates its own harsh weather.

But Peter has not finished. This question of womanly frailty, he seems to feel, needs more consideration. "I also think" (his essay style is really too pontifical, but then he is a rather pompous person at the moment). "I also think that a woman should be hard-working and still look fairly dainty when dressed right. On the other hand they should not be too dainty." (What a horrid word. He never learned it from me.) "We once had a helper who was too dainty and found housework for us too much and left."

Well that was not exactly what Shakespeare meant by Frailty: that his heroine would carry nothing heavier than a tea-tray. I often suspect that English-masters set essays for their own amusement and curiosity, as I would too if I had to mark twenty ill-spelt exercises on the same subject. And Peter's is so astonishingly ill-spelt that no one would believe it if I did not correct it, but copied it out as he has written it down.

I know I should not read his essay-book without him knowing but it is a temptation I seldom resist.

"The Apparel oft Proclaims the Man." (Clearly *no-one* could resist that.) "This is the case quite often," Peter considers. "If the man has a reckless character then he will dress without much thought, his tie halfway round his neck, his jacket open and all his hair in a muddle. But if on the other hand the man is quiet and good with matters in the house, they dress well and are tidy and neat with a bow-tie and a watch and chain. But as well as this you can also tell what nationality they are by their clothes. For instance you can tell an American from an Englishman because the former has a more dashing character and therefore wears things like tartan shirts and gaudy trousers."

I only hope that the dashing character makes up for the gaudy trousers, and that my American friends are not going to take offence. But what I really want to know is which of our acquaintance Peter considers quiet and good about the house, for certainly I can think of no-one we know who wears a watch and chain.

"Falstaff" it says on the next page, but here Peter is very brief. "Falstaff was a very big liar and went about a fair amount with the Prince of Wales."

I wonder whether their school version of Shakespeare is so bowdlerized that there is nothing else but that left of dear Falstaff, for most of him is scarcely suitable for small boys, if only because his low jokes take too much explaining to the ignorant. A new and quite unexpected amusement I have lately found, is reading the foot-notes of the boys' school Shakespeares. "Lust," says Shakespeare trenchantly, and a little star guides us to the foot-note at the bottom of the page. "Lust = unbridled passion." Then a few lines further down another star. "Appetite = ditto."

I had never realized before that clichés could have any real use, but I can see now that they are invaluable for wrapping up awkward facts in language so pompous and unmeaning that no one will ask any further questions. I can still remember my own shocked disapproval the first time I met Falstaff in full blood at the University. He was a nasty old man, I thought (for I was never prepared to admire simply because my betters told me to) and I said what I thought of him in essays which must have been as young and solemn and ridiculous as Peter's, and no doubt amused the setters in just the same way. It was a pity Shakespeare felt he must cater for the groundlings with such a low character —so I said in sanctimonious disapproval. He was not even amusing, so I pronounced (for Mercutio at that time was my idea of wit) and the plays would be better without him.

It was not exactly Falstaff's bawdiness which shocked me. As for that, the repartee of my hero Mercutio and his friend Romeo is as bawdy as any of Falstaff's, and I never minded *them* in the least (however surprising I privately thought it that Shakespeare should so mix up low jokes and high poetry). But Falstaff was different. Falstaff was a fat sweaty dirty disgusting old man, and that he should also be so unashamedly lascivious was more than I could stomach at my romantic eighteen years old. For at eighteen we have still a great deal more growing-up to do to become complete people, and I could no more see then than Peter can now that Falstaff is one of the great poetic creations.

But Peter is deaf to all poetry, deaf and unwilling to waste his time on frivolities.

"They've given us a poem to learn for Prep," he told us at tea-time. "I don't *mind* learning it—it's a nice lazy Prep and doesn't take a minute—but I do think it's an awful waste of time when there's so many important things to do."

I know all about Peter's opinion of poetry, but William is shocked by such blasphemy. For of all the people I have ever known, no-one quotes poetry so constantly and so enthusiastically as William. And quite certainly nobody quotes it so wrongly. Sometimes indeed, it is so remote from the original that no-one could possibly follow the thread, often it is only recognizable to my ear of faith and long habit, but generally it is a new and very Williamish paraphrase, near enough to what it should be to drive me to a frenzy of irritation trying to remember the original. Only very occasionally he produces it more or less as it was written.

Gray's "Elegy" is one of his more accurate pieces, and he recites a verse or two to Peter, to try him out as if with a kind of poetic litmus paper.

> *"Full many a gem of purest ray serene,*
>   *The dark unfathom'd caves of ocean bear:*
> *Full many a flower is born to blush unseen,*
>   *And waste its sweetness on the desert air."*

Peter listens attentively, withdrawn in thought for a minute or so while we all sit dumb round the table and watch him, waiting respectfully for his considered opinion.

"Well," he says at last, quietly and seriously, as if his judgment were immensely important to all of us. "There were flowers on the earth so many millions of years before there were any people to see them, that not many flowers even can have been seen by people anyway." He pauses and no-one speaks. "And flowers don't grow in deserts."

On Gray's "Elegy" there is no more to be said: as fact it is unreliable, as observation self-evident, and Peter is clearly disappointed. I watch him and wonder whether John will laugh at him, and whether Peter will mind, for he is perfectly serious in his considered judgment and quite without any sense of humour. Perhaps in time he will learn to laugh at himself, but not yet. Just now he is seldom amused except by deliberate jokes, and even those he is slow to understand. I sometimes hear John laboriously explaining the point of a story and Peter solemnly saying at last, "I see."

We need, I suppose, a certain cheerful poise and sense of balance before we can observe the harmless absurdities which surround us, with the kindly raillery which is a sense of humour. If we are uncertain or nervous or bewildered then we are not amused, and Peter is seldom amused. He is absent and preoccupied, and I am reminded often of an insect in a chrysalis. It is as if in his caterpillar condition of childhood he had swallowed down all the experience he needed for his development, and was now retired to some mysterious process of transformation which will change him from his slow grub-like state to an adult winged creature. Or so I hope, for I should be sad if he were never more confident than this.

In time he may even enjoy Gray's "Elegy," but meanwhile William had better do his quoting with John, who will keep him company and not mind the misquotations as I do. John indeed is none too accurate himself.

"Mine eyes have seen the glory of the coming of the Lord:
"He is trampling out the village where the grapes of wrath
are stored."

It is his favourite song of the moment for singing in the bath, and I wonder what he thinks it means? Though I agree that it does not matter and the rhythm's the thing. In any case the proper version makes scarcely more sense.

But John's chosen poem just now is "The Ancient Mariner." He is learning it by heart, quite undismayed by the page after page of verses. He writes poetry himself too, cheerful and vigorous verses which he hands round for our opinion.

SAILING—A SONNET

So he heads it, confident but mistaken about his verse forms.

A fair wind is blowing across the blue sea
And I am sailing home to tea.
After a day of boating upon the waves
Picnicing fishing and beautiful bathes.
The sails are a-billow, the anchor is up,
And now I am going home to sup.
My boat is a yacht called bonny Seagull
With a yellow mast and a green and red hull.
I've caught a trout and a couple of daice,
An eel and a minnow with a dirty face.
As I sail round the coast Ramsgate harbour I see
And I pull the rudder and swing to the lee.
The anchor in the water I drop with a splash
And let down the sails without even a crash.

How very vigorous his sailing is—splashing anchors, crashing sails (though not to-day) and lots of active exercise. (In the original version, but crossed out, the fourth line read "Picnicing *cricket* and beautiful bathes.") And how manly and dashing that "couple of daice"—though marine fauna is not really John's subject and he would do better to leave that sort of thing to Peter.

When I consider his idea of a jolly day however, I am rather disturbed by the number of meals he seems to want—tea, supper and an unspecified number of picnics. Do I not give him enough to eat, I wonder? "Ramsgate harbour I see"—and I felt sure the next rhyme would be tea. But no. He had looked forward to tea once already of course—it was the whole point of the day's jaunt I dare say—that he should go out boating upon the waves and sail home to tea rhyming with sea.

"Do you like it?" he asks expectantly. "I couldn't find a rhyme for 'up.' " No, so I can see, nor for "dance" either I should guess. And even the final crash has a rather forced feel about it. I wonder if he would like a rhyming dictionary in his Christmas stocking. But John is waiting for my opinion.

"Yes, I do like it. I think it's fine." "Fine," I feel, has the right breezy air. "Do you often write poetry?"

"Yes, I do. It doesn't take a minute. It's really very quick you know."

As always when I laugh at John I am not sure that he is not laughing with me at himself. For John is a social being, and the interest which Peter gives to abstract principles, John brings to his social relationships with other people. Not his personal or emotional relationships, which seem to be simple and satisfactory and take up little of his attention, but the way we all of us react to each other as social creatures. He seems to sense the atmosphere of the occasion.

Not that he consciously occupies himself with such nuances in his busy cheerful life. In so far as he has any idea at all about his relationships with other people, I think he would feel that our duty is to amuse each other. Thou shalt not bore thy neighbour. I think that would be high on the list of John's Commandments, second only to the more fundamental rule that we should all be happy. For John is not so much virtuous as kind: moved always to indignation by any suffering. He objects to cruelty and injustice not because they are wrong but because they are unkind. He is far more concerned that we should all be happy than that virtue should triumph. And since we all of us I suppose, see our problems in terms of our own standards, whether moral or material or aesthetic, and since for John the standards which matter are social, he sees his own problems in terms of social relationships.

"You know," he told me at tea not long ago, "when we went to our new school I *do* think you should've told us about not going off with strange men when they stop us in the street and talk to us." He looked at me kindly but seriously, taking me to task for neglecting what clearly seemed to John my social duty. I really *should* have warned him, so he implied, about the embarrassing difficulties of such encounters. But since the difficulties I foresee are far more serious than social embarrassment I looked at him with alarm.

Yet whatever had happened, I reflected, was long enough ago to be reported officially now as past experience, not even important enough to be worth concealing.

"Do they often stop you?" I asked, more curious now than alarmed, since here he was after all, calmly telling me about it. "Yes, they do," he said indignantly. "They're always stopping me. One said if I'd go with him we'd go down to the Docks and he'd take me over a ship. And another day a very smart one with a bowler hat and very clean gloves said he'd got two tickets for the theatre and wouldn't I like to go?"

John tells me this unexpected news in a voice of stern disapproval, though whether it is the invitations he disapproves of or my negligence as a parent, I cannot tell.

"And what did you say?" I asked, for I can see that with John's nice feeling for the social graces this would be the chief difficulty of the situation.

"Well, it was *most* embarrassing. After all, it was jolly decent of them to ask me to nice things like ships and the theatre. So I thanked them a lot you know, and said how kind to ask me and everything, but that really I'd got an *awful* lot of Prep that night, and I *must* be getting home now to get on with it. Then I always walk away as fast as ever I *can* without running till I'm round the corner."

Dear John, I can perfectly imagine him saying it, with the beautifully polite, almost courtly manner he assumes for formal occasions. I know exactly the tone of voice, very clear and impersonal, in a slightly higher key than his ordinary talking; and I have no doubt at all that he raised his cap and bid his strangers politely good-bye. Nor could I ever have taught him a more effective way of dealing with such situations, for there is no more impregnable defence after all, than detached formal courtesy in the wrong places. It is the cruellest weapon of all, especially when used against people who cannot use it back. It insults them in so many ways at once.

"It's all right now because we both know all about it. But we didn't at first." John is still scolding me in a kindly way. But I never would have warned them specifically against such hazards. They are both of them sensible people, and it has always seemed to me better to accept the very unlikely risk of serious trouble than to fill their minds deliberately with doubts and suspicions. Of course they tell each other horror stories at school—that I had relied on—but they know well enough about their own love of horrors to discount most of what their companions tell them in such round-eyed whispers. A solemn parental warning is a very different matter. If we who really know consider it as serious as *that*, then the ground they thought solid beneath their feet must be set with traps and pitfalls. How can they know? What about all the people they pass in the streets? Every day. All the time. Is it all horrid?

But if we say nothing—we grown-ups who know everything—there can be nothing they need to worry about; it will only be another difficulty like all the rest they have learned to deal with perfectly well by themselves. After all, in these affairs it is not what happens to us that matters, but whether we are upset by our experiences. And John is serenely unconcerned, only anxious now to reassure me after my scolding.

"But never mind, Dardy." He holds my hand in a kindly comforting way. "We both know *all* about it now. *You* needn't bother. We're always all right you know. Even if we're *very* late home you needn't *ever* bother."

For John has suddenly realized that this is an unexpected chance to discredit my irksome household rule that seven o'clock is late enough to come home from school, and that if they want to be later, then they must telephone and let me know. It is not that John really considers this unreasonable, but he likes to feel himself free and unhindered to arrange his own affairs, and he never lets a chance go by to undermine the rules which restrict his independence.

I can foresee that John and I will always be on these pull-Devil-pull-baker terms as long as we live together. There will always be something I insist on and John resists, if only on the excellent general principle of Up-Freedom-and-Down-with-all-Restrictions. It is fortunate that he is fundamentally good-natured and bears me no ill-will. Though I suppose I shall not always win. I can scarcely expect to harness two boys with my nursery apron-strings when they grow as tall as I am. I only hope I shall be as good-natured about my dwindling authority as John is now about his limited independence.

"But I *would* like to go round the Docks." Virtue may be triumphant but vice is baited with attractions which it seems to John a pity to miss. "Will *you* take us round one day instead?"

John looks at me with pleading eyes, as if there were nothing in the whole world he wanted more than this visit to the Docks he has only just thought of. All right, I tell him, we will go in a boat one day in the summer, or if he likes he can come with William and me on one of our evening drives round the town.

For sometimes, on summer evenings, when the air is soft and the traffic of the day is over, we go out to look at London. Go to Chiswick to walk by the river, or up to the Hampstead-Highgate hills to look down through the trees on the endless city spread out blue below. Or if the light has gone, we drive down to the City to see the great organic mass of the Tower miraculously floodlit, and over it the full moon floating, tangled in trees. Mostly it is East we go, to the City and beyond, for there, when one comes to know it, is the romantic heart of London.

So we can go to the Docks for John if he likes, but he will have to get used to our odd way of travelling. For although William has lived all his life in London, he is almost as lost here as he is in Paris, he lacks completely any sense of direction. I often wonder what the town would look like if he drew a plan of it for a stranger. Like nothing at all, quite certainly, that anyone else would recognize as London. And here, since he has no Arc de Triomphe to climb to, he has never found any satisfactory way for checking his direction. The river, so he used to say when first I knew him, the river was the thing. The thing to steer by. The Thames, he said, flowed West to East: one side was North London, the other side South. You must only take care, so he used to assure me, not to cross the river, either over or under, without noticing. Otherwise you got lost. Got *lost*, he said, as if that were something rare and seldom and not the usual background of all our journeys together. But in those days I knew no better and listened to what he said. And if you were not sure which side of the river you were on, so he would go on to tell me (and indeed we were seldom sure of anything about our journey) then, he said, you went to a bridge and looked which way the current was running and then you could work it out.

But the London Thames flows round in circles, as anyone can see from the map. It is only on the unfairly simple plan of the Underground that we imagine it flows from West to East. And as for the current—a dead dog, so they say, drowned in the Pool of London, will wash up and down on the tide under London Bridge seven times before it is carried out to sea. It was William who told me, one day when we met, leaning over the bridge, watching the current flow perversely upstream. For certainly it *was* upstream it was flowing, not down, since there was the dome of Saint Paul's, not to be mistaken.

Then he would buy a compass, said William, impatient with the river's vagaries but cheerfully full of ideas, and he would fix it to the dash-board of his motor-car and then we should always know which way we were going. But we never do know, even now after years of going about, we know scarcely better than we did at first. It has always been one of the delights of travelling with William, and our journeys have changed very little. In the beginning we start out, and in the end we get there, but as to where we may go inbetween—about that there is no way of knowing. Certainly we both of us have our own familiar routes about the town—to shops or hospitals or museums or libraries or the houses of friends. We use them constantly, link them up to reach new places, branch off from them unwillingly, follow them without thinking because they are familiar; even though there must be far quicker ways than going round three sides of a square as we often do. It is only that we cannot be bothered to learn them. We can drive the ways we know without thinking, and neither of us minds driving as long as we can think of something else.

There are times, however, when no possible combination of our routes will take us where we want to go, and then quite simply we set off into the blue in a suitable general direction. There is no planning of routes beforehand, no pulling up under street lamps to work out our way on the map. William has no patience to stop and ask the way of passers-by. ("They never know," he says. "They're always strangers here themselves." And so they always are: it is one of the mysteries—how the people we meet in a strange place never seem to belong there. I can only think that the ones who do live there are all indoors, as we are here.) So William drives on simply, lost but confident, making of the outing, not simply a journey from place to place, but an impromptu tour of London.

He turns right or left as the fancy takes him, liking the look of an old street or the green of an open space, catching sight of an interesting unknown spire over the roof-tops—and we *must* go and look. And sooner or later, since he has lived here all his life, we come to a road he knows. Though even then it is not simple. For off we go, as often as not, in the wrong direction and are lost again; for William will never turn round simply and go back the opposite way, but find some side-street laid out, so he trustingly believes, merely to take us back again in a loop to the road we have just left.

It means we make quite astonishingly complicated journeys to near-by places, we discover snug corners of London we should never find if we knew the way. We cross the river by one bridge and back by the next (for we know better now than to bother with the river), come to a stop in the yards of warehouses, on the edge of docks, or in strange dark cul-de-sacs where friendly Cockney night-watchmen greet us in surprise.

They are journeys I never tire of, exploring worlds not realized with a companion whose confident curiosity keeps at bay the misgivings which still too easily overwhelm me alone in the town. They are journeys I would never make by myself, for the city is still not reliably friendly beyond our familiar village. It is neither friendly nor hostile, but indifferent, denying all reassurance, leaving us defenceless in the sinister darkness which from time to time shuts out the sun and cheerful daylight views, so that in the landscape of our lives we can see nothing any more but strangeness and dread. It is when we stand alone in strange city places that we wait for the bombs to fall.

WELL. WHAT NEWS TODAY?"
It is tea-time and the children home from school, and it has somehow become a family convention that when they come in for tea we should all for a time sit idly round the table and exchange our various news of the day in an atmosphere of general goodwill. Or rather I am idle, merely drinking tea, but the children have the very serious business of eating to attend to before they are ready to sit back in their chairs and gossip. In the early stages of tea there is no conversation, only a purposeful clatter of knives on plates and mugs on saucers; but when the slices of toast and treacle have disappeared, and the tomatoes and raw carrots and the cakes and biscuits and mugs of milk (for their palates are as childish as ever, even if their minds are not) when they feel at last they can eat no more, and there is in any case very little left to eat, then they lean back in their chairs as benign and genial as diners after a good dinner, ready to take their part in the tea-time entertainment. It is the social occasion of the family day, a peaceful expansive interlude of leisure between the crowded journey home from school and the dreary business of settling down to the evening's homework.

Three Years of Growing

"Well. What news today?"

"Nothing really," Peter says, but he does his best. "Except that today was the day we have a lecture in School Prayers. They talk to us for a quarter of an hour, but it's *never* the sort of things I want to know. Today it was called 'Why we pray.' You can't listen to things like *that* for a quarter of an hour. *No-one* could." Peter is indignant. "I wish they'd sometimes give us lectures on butterflies instead, or early man, or cricket, or what books to read." But Peter seems to feel that this kind of grumbling can scarcely count as news, and there is something else he saved from his day.

"There's new trends in Arabia," he tells us, "I read it in some-one's newspaper sitting next to me on the bus on the way home. But people never let you read their newspapers, do they? They always turn it so's you just can't see. So I don't know what trends are. Dardy, what're trends?"

I explain seriously, since parents must, but I think how much more interested I should be if trends were some kind of antelope running swift as shadows across desert sands, and how much pleasanter it would be for all of us if they were.

John is not interested in Middle East politics, and it is his turn now.

"Well," he says reflectively, making a mental survey of his day, considering what might amuse the tea-table, passing over no doubt in silence the many things he now considers it more suitable for parents not to know. "Well," says John, with a half-swallowed chuckle which warns me not to be taken in by his bland expression, "I *know* you'll be pleased to hear that I'm do-ing better at school this turn." They still call it turn as a private joke, even now that they know better. "This turn and next turn" they used to think it was, as if each school term were a game they joined in to win prizes, a kind of school roulette played three times a year.

"I'm still not wonderful at arithmetic," John goes on. "I'm

bottom actually. But you'll be glad to know I've gone up in the football class. Last year I was no good. Last year I couldn't run. I was bottom of the class at running. But in the holidays I put in a lot of running practice you know. I ran all about, here and there, and so now I'm better at football."

Whether this nonsense is really for our general amusement, or only to keep parents' minds off the arithmetic I cannot tell. And in any case it is my turn now.

News is not one of the things I am good at, being too much in the house; but to-day I have something far better than any of theirs.

This morning, I tell them, I went to Hamley's toy-shop, which was cram-full of people doing their shopping early for Christmas. Peter and John have been to Hamley's, they know about the crowds and also about the loudspeakers which call out the names of lost children brought to the office, and ask for the mothers to fetch them. And while I was there to-day, I tell them, the loudspeakers suddenly called out "Mrs. Wilson. Calling Mrs. Wilson. Her husband has lost her. Will she please go and find him. He's on the second floor, at the toy train counter."

This the children find enormously funny—the right and proper debunking of grown-ups, and they both rock backwards and forwards in hilarious laughter. But alas, I cannot often provide such treasure, and they think much more highly of William's sense of humour than mine. To-day he is telling them about the toys he used to have as a boy, "a wonderful book which told you how to make a model of Cologne Cathedral with cigar-boxes. But what it *didn't* tell you was how to get enough cigar-boxes. Hundreds and hundreds it needed. And when you got to the tower and there weren't enough to finish, you waited outside Papa's study door I suppose, and collected cigar-boxes as he kept throwing them out one after the other all day long."

This is the standard they expect of William, for he has a seemingly endless collection of little stories which he can produce at a moment's notice to suit any occasion. "Did I ever tell you about the man . . . ?" he asks. "Do you know about the dog . . . ?" "Have I told you the story about this that or the other?"

"No. No. You haven't," the children are always quick to assure him, looking forward to the joke as if it were a chocolate held tantalizingly under their noses. And they are right. William never has told it before; his stories are always new and delightful and as innocent as nursery-rhymes. In our confidential moments he assures me that he has told me the same stories often, and that I never remember: that he need only wait a day or two and he can tell me them all over again as good as new. And he takes my arm and says I am a good wife.

But he need not praise me. For me they *are* new. I never have been able to remember funny stories, and I wait for them just as eagerly as the children. Where he gets them from I cannot imagine, nor certainly how he remembers them, for they are buried treasure I never knew anything of in all our married life till now, and it seems very odd that I married in my twenties a young man who would produce in his forties a wealth of stories to amuse our growing sons.

"That's a pun," said Peter, delighted that for once he had seen the joke before John.

"You don't know what a pun is," I said to encourage him, though quite clearly he does.

"Yes we do," John assures me. "Once upon a time there was a wounded man, and he knew he was going to die, and he was always making jokes. And they asked him if he felt better, and he said 'No. I don't. Ask me tomorrow and I'll be a *grave* man.' That's a pun."

Goodness me. I suppose I must have quoted it for them at some time, "Not so deep as a well, nor so wide as a church-door," for I always remember with affection my early hero Mercutio. But what a precious household they live in, poor things.

Tea now is long since over. No-one can think of any more

news either real or invented, and the boys realize they cannot put off much longer the homework which I still cannot remember to call Prep.

"We've to write out the story of Helen of Troy," John announces.

"I don't even know it," Peter tells him with a certain scorn, and I can see that Greek myths for Peter come close after poetry as a frivolous waste of time: quite useless as sources of serious information. But John is quick to see that here is a rare opportunity to instruct his older brother, and he gives us a modern version of the story in vigorous schoolboy slang. It is all very dramatic and full of high-speed action like his comics, and the only part which puzzles him is whether or not Paris was ever *married* to Helen. It seems a finicky consideration in the circumstances, but John likes to know where he is in these delicate situations. I remember how well "artificial wife" would have described either Helen or Oenone—or both for that matter—but "artificial" is no longer a word they use, it is as dead now as last year's fashions in hats. And John has not finished.

"Then Paris got wounded by a poisoned arrow, and he went back to Oenone to heal him, and she was jolly decent about it and was just going to, when he started talking about Helen, and then she was so fed up that she let him die."

There is a pause while Peter considers this somewhat unheroic ending.

"I think that was a bit thick."

"No it wasn't." Clearly John disapproves of adulterers, whatever the temptations. "It served him jolly well right."

Neither of them can be bothered to go on with the argument, and we all sit idle and floppy on our chairs until at last I rouse myself to make movements of getting up—brisk determined movements meant to be infectious, for John and Peter really must get up too and help me clear the table, then settle down to work.

But it is more amusing to tell poor Oenone's story than to write it, and besides, the kitchen has a warm and comfortable atmosphere of too much tea which does not help with the homework. John sits turning over the pages of a tattered blue exercise book labelled comprehensively History and Geography.

"I can't think *where* this came from," he tells me in a superior voice. "It's *frightfully* old. It's one I had *ages* ago when I was very young."

I realize that "ages ago" is probably last year in his first term at Prep school. "When I was very young," children say, and "I can just remember—a long time ago." And we laugh at them because we no longer remember our own childhood. But our minds reckon time by changes in ourselves, not by dates on a calendar, and we do as much of our growing-up before we are ten years old as we do between ten and dying. It is as if the adult state were a wide plateau which we climb to in childhood and adolescence, and on the steep slopes up, a journey of a hundred yards may change our mental landscape more than travelling a whole mile along the level ground above. "A long time ago," the children say, and what they mean is that in a year's climbing the view has changed completely. "When I was very young," they say, in pitying wonder at how little of the world they used to see, down there among the foothills.

Yet though they may live with us and be free and friendly, parents can know very little of how their children's minds are changing. It is not that they are secretive or do not want us to know, but they do not understand what there is to tell, their whole consciousness is involved in the development, there is no detached observer to assess and report, either to us or to themselves. When they are very young we can see for ourselves, if we look carefully and impartially, a great deal of what is going on, but as they grow older they become more separate and complex, they develop in new ways inherent in themselves, become new individuals whom we cannot necessarily understand.

John is still turning over the pages of his Geography and History notebook and waiting for me to take some interest. It starts off simply and confidently with a clear statement of the theme which recurs throughout like a chorus: "Istanbul's other name is Constantinople." Why this should be the beginning of all History and Geography I cannot see, but of all the snippets of information which seem to have been showered down on John's head like ticker-tape, this is the one which caught his fancy: that a domed and distant city has two quite different names, each as magical and mysterious as the other: that Istanbul's other name is Constantinople.

We have learned the chorus now and we can begin:

> Columbus listened to sea-stories at Genoa.
> Athens has ruined temples.
> Naples has Vesuvius behind it.
> Patros sends currants to England.

It seems that at nine years old Geography is best learned in a series of half-line statements. History is distinguished by a different-coloured ink.

"School in 1850 was not like ours. For one thing it began at seven o'clock."

There is no comment and no further information. That must have been all that John thought worth recounting of his History lesson, for the next page is Geography again—a map of Australia and a drawing of a kangaroo with a very surprised baby looking out of a kind of handbag in front. Underneath it says, "Istanbul's other name is Constantinople."

Then John grows more companionable and talks to us confidentially. "If I were an Australian Bushman I would watch the strange and wonderful birds, catch and tame ostriches, kill troublesome snakes and catch kangaroos. I would go to New Guinea and see the beautiful waterfalls there."

It sounds much more like a Londoner on holiday than a poor

depressed Bushman, and are there *really* ostriches in Australia? In any case John has finished with the Antipodes (except for reminding us again about Istanbul), and the next two pages are History—labelled drawings of weapons: daggers, clubs, swords and "foreign swords" in endless variety. And each has its own "shieth, shief"—then he tries again—"sheith," a hard word to spell and he gives it up for the moment to tell us about Dermot. "Dermot was strong and he fought long and hard a battle with Edward. But little by little step by step, he got on top and won the battle." Underneath is a drawing of Dermot (or perhaps it is Edward), dressed in a check suit which I suppose is chain-mail, holding a sword in one hand and a spear in the other, and at his feet another array of unlikely-looking weapons. But no sheaths this time to bother the spelling.

The next page is more succinct, with no attempt at drama or purple passages. "A Crusader is a man who went to the Holy Land. In the end they lost."

After that there is page after page of reasonable facts about pilgrims and Thomas à Becket and Domesday Book (and Istanbul's other name of course), with only here and there an original spelling to enliven the lesson. Jurusulum looks somehow sullen, and Ekscheker altogether too spiky. But always there is the same interest in weapons.

"The sword of a King has a lovely jewelled handle and is extra sharp." Then another picture with its label. "A Roman sword and sheath." Right at last.

From time to time there are sudden surprising statements which I think must be History lessons. "My house is a cave built high up in a wall. It is a bit cold at times, but I think it is very nice." Then almost without pause "The Roman Wall reached from one sea to the other. I expect it was very hard work not only building the wall, but keeping out the Picts and Scots. In the end the Romans had to go home."

John has a ruthless way I notice, of finishing off his characters quickly when he is tired of them. But now he turns over a new page and starts off with a flourish.

"This is a play about a Night's Son becoming a Night." (Father is called N. and son is called N.S.)

Scene 1

N.S.   Father. When am I to become a Night?

N.   Next week my boy.

N.S.   Hooray.

Scene 2 (*next week*)

N.   Now do not forget to be courteous.

N.S.   No, Father.

Scene 3

ANOTHER NIGHT   Oho my boy. Are you the new page I wanted?

N.S.   Yes, Sir.

What happened after that we never know, for with this show of courtesy John loses interest in the theatre, and off we go again amassing information. "Constantinople's other name is Istanbul." We had guessed it might be, but at least it makes a change the other way round.

"Domesday Book was to tell William about the country. The people were very grumpy about it."

"The date that William the Conqueror came to England was 1066."

We knew that too, but it soon gets more controversial.

"Stonehenge is thought to be an early English church." "A token was a little badge that pilgrims liked to buy." Then comes the Istanbul-Constantinople refrain, but for the last time, for John has drawn a careful line through it, crossed it out at last as redundant.

Without the chorus however, Geography and History lose their interest. It was the words John liked I suppose, since he has always collected strange words as Peter collects strange butter-

flies, to say and savour them at odd moments like sniffing a flower
in our buttonhole. And in this notebook which has lost its chorus
there is only one more entry: a surprising and very Johnish statement about the tastes of kings.

"Kings had bards to play to them. They loved to go into battle. They loved to sing and go to the fair." Certainly John would
go to the fair if he were king, and fill the house with singing and
good company, and go off to battle from time to time for hilarious exercise with his friends.

To-night however he must do his homework, and we are not
getting on at all. He is half-lying across the table, drawing separate pictures of some private strip-cartoon on consecutive pages
of his Latin grammar. His eyes are indigo-blue in the lamp-light,
and his cheeks are the living pink which the French must mean
by *incarnat*. For although his feet have grown awkwardly large
and his knees big and bony, John still keeps the face he has had
since a baby, soft and round and delicious.

Indeed they are both of them now at the same stage of growing-up as the ducklings we feed on the lake in the park on summer evenings; fluffy still, but with their adult feathers already
showing through the down, an awkward and endearing transition. Although John learns Latin now, he scribbles down the
verbs he must remember in the margins of comics, and Peter
makes models of Stonehenge in biscuits on the kitchen table. And
despite a consciousness of their new adult status as responsible
Londoners, they are still as playful as puppies at the least encouragement. Even Peter, the solemn and thoughtful, is danced off
into gaiety by John's infectious high spirits. They lark about (no
other word so exactly describes the good-tempered romping of
boys), they shout and sing, and play the old childish games they
have played for years. Just now they collect old telephone di-
rectories to make paper darts, hundreds and hundreds of darts:
flying across the kitchen, planing down the staircase, carefully
aimed along the hall and swooping through doorways, and spe-

cial darts cunningly folded so that they come back to the thrower like boomerangs. As a game it is irresistible, and sooner or later everyone joins in. I have even invented a new-style dart of my own, which flies with a peculiar swooping motion and gives me the greatest satisfaction.

The children delight too in practical jokes. Coming in late at night, William and I are greeted by white paper skeletons hanging on invisible threads from the bannisters of the floor above. We find trick tea-spoons in the sugar, match-boxes which will not open, pools of mock ink on the carpet. And on days when they finish their homework early, the boys spend busy evenings engrossed in making booby-traps to surprise me in their bedrooms. Down the stairs all evening come whispers, giggles, stifled bursts of laughter. When they hear me coming (for it is only fair to make a noise), there is sudden frenzied activity—closing of doors and bundlings under beds, so that they can be ready to greet me, nonchalantly and self-consciously doing nothing when I reach the top of the stairs.

They are good-natured however, and seem to bear me no ill-will. Their pleasure is not in my discomfiture but in their own ingenuity, it is only that they must have me as the necessary victim. But because they know I am jumpy and start at shadows, they pin up an obliging notice on the door to warn me before I come into their rooms. TRAPS IN ACTION it says, and I open the door gingerly, ready for surprises. But all the knobs are tied together, and all the doors around me mysteriously open at the same time. I step cautiously inside, but a dust-sheet floats down from the ceiling and envelopes me, and as I struggle free, hundreds of glass marbles pour thundering down a ramp and spread out across the floor in front of me in a rolling coloured fan. "Thousands of marbles. Billions of marbles. Infinity marbles," John chants in ecstasy from the bed, hugging his arms round his chest and rocking backwards and forwards.

Nor is that the end. Paper darts swoop down from nowhere,

balloons burst at my approach, string pendulums swing across the room in front of my nose. And somewhere in the background Peter and John squirm and giggle with delight, for in their play they are still surprisingly childish, in relief I suppose from the constant hard work of growing-up.

Boys of this age (and girls too perhaps, but we have no daughters) are cheerful company: thumping upstairs, clattering about their bedrooms, splashing in the bath, scuffling and shouting. They are like a healthy wind blowing through the house, boisterous and rough and tiresome, but quite without malice or sulks or any ill-feeling. They bring with them a bracing holiday atmosphere of open-air and sea-breezes, and are no doubt good for all of us. Certainly they are good for me, who left to myself am always in danger of arranging a single perfect lily in a green glass vase, hanging a Chinese silk painting over my bed, and living as neatly and exquisitely as a cat. For I move too quietly left alone for long, grow over-squeamish and disturbed by shadows. And it is no use being over-sensitive with a house and family to deal with. Most household days can only be got through by plunging in vigorously and not bothering too much about the niceties. A household needs an exhaustingly large supply of rough peasant energy simply to keep it running at all.

Yet the children now are growing up fast. Peter especially is emerging from his chrysalis-stage to realize with delight that growing-up is a journey into an adult world where he begins to feel himself at home at last. The childhood he has never had much gift for enjoying is almost over, and his life ahead, so he seems to feel, will be very much more to his liking. Perhaps we are all of us most fitted by our personalities to some certain stage of our lives, and it is that time in our development that we remember always with the greatest happiness; not because the events which happened to us were particularly fortunate, but because we were then most suited to our life. Perhaps it is why two different people will look back on the same period with pleasure or with horror—their schooldays it may be, or life in the army.

Certainly it has not suited Peter to be a young child. It has been a time of bewildered waiting, of joining conscientiously and without gaiety in the childish life about him. It is as if, not being suited to childhood, his life till now had been a long voyage across an ocean whose watery movements he neither enjoyed nor understood. Where John has been a confident sailor, Peter I think, has been haunted by fear of shipwreck. But now he is reaching the shore, a land creature on dry land at last.

Of course the country ahead is strange and difficult: there will be storms on land as there were at sea, and fearful forests of darkness. But Peter lately is alive with a new self-confidence; as if for the first time he felt the ground reassuringly solid beneath his feet, and no longer any danger of drowning. The difficulties ahead (for Peter has never been an optimist) will be comprehensible; he will be able to find the way out for himself in terms he can understand.

For the first time now he begins to be light-hearted. Not simply the animal high-spirits which he caught infectiously from John, but privately gay beneath his grave and quiet manner.

"There was a Frenchman at school to-day," he told me at tea-time, "and he talked French to us all the time. But you know I couldn't understand a word he said—he'd got such a *dreadful* accent."

I looked at him in surprise. Had he really meant it to be absurd? But this time quite certainly he had. He smiled at me with the oddest mixture of amusement at his own joke, and astonishment at his new-found powers of joking. It is almost as if a stranger had joined us for tea.

Perhaps now he may do better at school, which would certainly please him. For he has been till now a mediocre plodder, disappointed in his own keenly-felt limitations. "I'm third in my class," he told me, "and I'll *never* be any more, because I'm just not any *better* than that. The two boys who beat me are just cleverer than I am, that's all. If I ever *did* beat them it would only be an accident, and not fair. It wouldn't mean I'm cleverer than they are, because I'm *not*."

He was sad but resigned, and certainly no amount of teaching Latin and Greek will turn Peter into a Classical scholar, nor will his French accent ever be less than excruciatingly English. But perhaps he may turn out to be a scientist who has not yet started science.

"Write an Essay on Birds." His English master set it as a subject for homework, and if he expected little stories about feathered friends he must have been surprised by Peter's eagerly written pages.

"The bird is a very odd animal, and it is not on the same route as us" (I only hope the English master knows about charts of evolution). "So even though it is warm-blooded like us, it lays eggs which hatch out and grow into adults, in this way it is like the Reptiles, but it is warm-blooded so it can't be. Well the truth is that the birds are descendents from the Reptiles. The oldest birds are very odd, they have teeth, and claws on their elbows, and most strange—a tail. The birds to-day have a crop to eat with instead of teeth, and feathers for the tail, but nothing left to show that at one time they had claws on their elbows. But now let's see what birds are like inside.

"The chicken is a delicacy and it is often eaten at parties. The breast is thought to be the best bit because it is the muscle that works the wing, which has to be very strong because the bird depends on it mainly to escape its enemies with. So there is always a nice lot of it." Peter finishes off with satisfaction, for he is something of a gourmet always.

"I myself," he remarks disapprovingly in another essay on the Mount Everest Expedition, "I myself do not think the people of the Expedition have done much to find out what the Abominable Snowman is, because they have all been too busy trying to get to the top of Mount Everest to think about it properly. What I would like is to have photos of all the animals' footprints known and living to-day. Then all the new animals they found we could look them up and see what they are most like."

What a priggish essay style my elder son has, and how very earnest. But one thing the English master must surely realize by now is that Peter's heart is not in English composition but in the Natural History Museum at South Kensington. For Peter it is the Promised Land waiting to welcome him, a fascinating and comprehensible world where his particular intellectual curiosity is unexpectedly satisfied. These are the childhood interests which he thought were his alone, but here quite serious grown-ups also study the holes in skulls, sensible adults share his enthusiasm and arrange all manner of pleasures for his delight and instruction. The Natural History Museum is his holiday province, and on any free time in London he hurries off to spend the day entranced till closing-time beneath its somewhat surprising roof.

Not that he ever calls it the Natural History Museum. That would be childish. For they are both of them at the stage of growing-up (it lasted me well through the University and beyond) when everything possible must be referred to by initials or abbreviations. And if the abbreviations can also be mispronounced, then that seems to them the height of witty sophistication.

So it is to the "Nat. Hiss. Muss." that Peter goes off with such single-minded eagerness; and sometimes I go with him, partly because I too like museums, and partly to share his heartening enthusiasm in his new intellectual kingdom. For he explores with vivid delight this new realm of the mind, finding his own way about the logical country of scientific method. It is as if, dumb till now, he had suddenly been given a language to think in, to explain his pleasure in the world about him.

The Natural History Museum is a half-way house to science, science on the human level of existence as distinct from the movements of galaxies or the structure of atoms. And since it is most carefully arranged for lay ignorance, here even I am safely within my depth. With no science at all I can enjoy this orderly plan of the background and origins of our human lives. I have only to make the effort.

But my appetite for facts is a mere invalid's toying with food beside Peter's voracious gobble. The theories I puzzle to understand are for Peter self-evident demonstrations. He is quick and confident as he has never been before, as if in this Promised Land he had found what he unconsciously needed: ground where he can root and grow to his full development.

Quite soon he goes off without me, like an eager dog broken free of its restraining leash, a small purposeful figure in the vast building, hurrying from one gallery to the next, engrossed, intent, oblivious alike of me, and his surroundings, and the near approach of tea-time.

I settle down to wait for him, exhausted both in mind and body, sitting patiently on a hard bench while he goes off on a last enthusiastic expedition to some far corner of his new world. I consider the astonishing architecture which encloses me. Carved birds cling to the leafy mouldings of the arches, strange creatures peer out at us from the foliage at the tops of pillars, a string of stone monkeys climbs high up the wall and across the roof. And beneath these surprising architectural fancies drift preoccupied children, in ones or twos mostly, but sometimes whole groups together—nearly always children, come of their own accord in their holiday time. They seem to me very *young* children to be taking so adult an interest in serious subjects, but it is always surprising how intelligent young children are; as if man's intellect, being our speciality, had only to develop through the brief background stages of man's short existence, while the emotional life we share with the other animals must pass through the slow evolution of our long biological history in the animal kingdom.

Yet looking at the models of brains in cases, at the astonishingly fast increase in size between the early primates and man, no-one could help wondering whether we are not still only at the beginning of our intellectual development, whether we have not still a great distance to go from our present state, so that the difference between our own and man's future brain may perhaps be as wide eventually as the difference now is between our own emotions and a cow's. Perhaps in time we may evolve such highly-developed intellects that it will take our future descendents as long to reach their full intellectual growth as it now takes us with our emotions. Indeed it seems a waste, when we live so long, that at eighteen years or so we should reach our highest peak of intelligence.

Perhaps the scientific mind is the new and immature growth of man's intellect. Perhaps the scientists are pushing forward not only the growing fringes of man's knowledge, but the new growth of his brain as well. Mathematics for instance is surely a new abstract way of thinking which man has developed. And in time perhaps, the sciences will become a true education of man's spirit, as only the humanities have been till now. For if the sciences so far do not show man at his full human stature, that is only perhaps because in the alphabet of science we are probably no further yet than ABC, and no-one can spell out anything very profound with only three letters.

But I am bored. I am tired of waiting for Peter, tired of sitting on a bench in front of models of brains and vaguely philosophizing. I wish he would come back, and I feel that if I have to wait much longer I shall begin to dislike him. I will go and look for him, I decide, but where to start looking I have no idea, for he has taken the whole museum to his heart and finds new treasures in remotest corners.

In front of the elephant's skeleton a little girl is dragging her father by the hand and desperately insisting— "Yes I know. But where's its *trunk?* I know there's everything else, but where's its trunk? There *must* be a trunk."

They laugh at her and no-one tells.

"Where's its trunk? Where's its trunk?" She is angry and anxious in almost equal proportions. I can see that for some reason the trunk matters, and I wonder whether she will cry. Peter and I would have told her about noses and things, but then Peter and I are earnest serious creatures, we are always ready to explain. We are only surprised when people are not interested in such fascinating subjects. But just now I am not interested either. I want to go home. It is more than half an hour since Peter left me, and if I thought he had any money for bus-fare I would leave him to get back alone.

Perhaps if I go and look for him somewhere else? But I know how elusive he is in this great tank of knowledge where he darts out of sight like a fish. But still, if I stroll about he may catch sight of me and decide to come back, like a dog on a country walk.

I loiter in likely places, at the cross-roads of the different galleries, by the cases of early man, and in front of the blue whale which swims enormous and immobile in its walled-in sea of air. But the blue whale is really too extravagantly large, and as a Londoner conscious always of the housing shortage I am shocked at such waste of space. Of course they must keep the whale, but in its hollow inside there must surely be plenty of room to lay out a self-contained flat as its invisible entrails. Though perhaps the authorities have thought of it already. Perhaps a modern-style Jonah and his wife already live snugly with all modern conveniences in the belly of Hell. Perhaps every morning before we come a cleverly camouflaged door opens in its side, and out steps a neat little man with a bowler hat and a rolled umbrella, who goes off to the City in a bus he catches at the stop outside the museum.

I examine the whale as it swims serene and noncommittal about its inside arrangements. That crack running up its nicely-painted sea-blue flank—surely that could be a blue front door? If I watch, perhaps soon (for it is nearly closing-time thank goodness, and then Peter *must* come back), perhaps the door will open cautiously, and his wife will set it ajar to let out the smell of onions she is frying for his supper.

I am interrupted by a bell ringing somewhere far off down the echoing corridors, a most melodious bell, for I know it means closing-time. And there begins a general drift of figures towards the main doors, as if a plug had been pulled out of a sink and we were all drawn out with the emptying water like tea-leaves. The children go reluctantly, lingering as they pass their favourite cases, but I am not reluctant at all, I am delighted. Perhaps after all I will not scold Peter for leaving me so long, but only make sure he has bus-fare the next time we come.

Certainly I will not scold him I decide as he rushes up, vividly alive, beaming with contentment at the thought of all the new treasures of information he has mentally collected.

"Wonderful," he says, with a great sigh of satisfaction. "I found a whole new piece of museum I never knew about before."

But museums for me at the moment are deserts of discomfort. I shall not be happy till I am sitting in my motor-car and driving home as fast as I can go. The very sight of the shabby old car cheers my spirits, a friendly familiar shape waiting patiently outside in the entrance-yard like a faithful animal.

"The poor thing," I say protestingly to Peter. "How would you like to be kept waiting all this time in the cold?"

It is the nearest I can bring myself to scolding so enthusiastic a companion as Peter is to-day. But I need not worry, he is impervious to such mild innuendo.

"O, I don't know," he says airily. "I expect it does it good. It hardens it off you know, ready for winter nights." And he chuckles, delighted with his newly-sprouting sense of humour. It is as if he had suddenly found he could do a new trick which he had never known how to attempt before.

Three Years of Growing

We climb into the car and I shut the doors with satisfaction, feeling myself at home and comfortably at my ease in the small travelling room which is a motor-car. Peter is in most hilarious high spirits and eager to be off. "Go on," he urges me as I wait for the hesitant cold engine to grow more confident before we launch out into the river of traffic. "Go on. Choke it. Clutch it. Throttle it. Strangle it." He pauses. "Why are all the words about cars so nasty to them, poor things?"

So they are, though I had never noticed it before. But since it was men who invented the words, and since men's cars are always "she," the only explanation I can think of is quite unsuitable for eleven years old.

"I don't know," I say meekly, "I don't even know what they mean when you do them." Which is quite true: I know nothing at all about motor-cars except how to drive them. But no doubt Peter will soon be eager to explain the whole thing, and I shall have to listen and learn at last.

Now we are off, sidling through the gates and into the hurrying traffic to make our way home through the evening rush-hour of central London. There are various ways of driving across London. We can keep to the main roads if we like, the obvious thorough-fares marked on the map, and which people use who do not know the town. At night these roads do well enough, but in the day-time they are best avoided, too choked with traffic and checked with traffic-lights, long journeys of frustration. And superimposed on this map of main-roads is another network of back-streets and side-roads, the ways the taxis use to travel about the town and avoid the traffic. The taxis and the people who know London, for because these are not the obvious ways for strangers, not roads we would pick out on a map, the traffic in these streets is not the main-road hotch-potch of buses and vans and cars unused to the town, but experienced traffic which knows its way about: professional taxis, large cars with chauffeurs, and indigenous local cars. And on these side-road routes about London the driving is different. On the main-roads the traffic is like an indiscriminate too-large class of children, and the pace is the pace of the slowest; but on these other unmarked routes the pace is the pace of the taxis, the picked pupils trained in their own special subject. For taxis are the professional athletes of the driving world, and they are always in training. No wonder we ordinary drivers find them pro-voking. They are too quick and too skilled and far too energetic. To keep up with them we must give our whole mind to the driving, which is tiresome; but if we travel by their particular routes then we *must* keep up or they bully us. We must drive close up to the one in front and not be nervous of the one behind almost touching our bumpers, or the ones which drive along each side of us without an inch to spare whenever they think the road is wide enough to take us all abreast. We must not dawdle, we must never hesitate for a second, we must shoot away at traffic-lights, swing neatly round corners side by side like skating and without taking the smallest slice of anyone else's share of road, we must follow them as they dart through gaps in the traffic so narrow that I would edge through slowly and care-fully if only I were by myself. But no. I must keep up. And if I hesitate, they blow their horns at me—the smallest discreetest little poops certainly, but irresistibly compelling.

For taxis are dreadful bullies, friendly and genial, but bullies for all that. Whenever I get caught up in a posse of taxis I feel like the victim in a film surrounded by a posse of gangsters. They hustle me across Mayfair and down Saint James's to the London Library, and I know I must keep up whether I like it or not. Certainly they grin down at me when we stop at traffic-lights, surveying my muddy car with non-committal interest. "Blimey," they say, "could do with a nice cup of tea while we're waiting," and they wink at me companionably and rub their hands energetically in the cold. But the moment the lights change they hurry me on; I must leap away on the yellow without waiting for the green, must speed down clear patches of road and rush across London as if we were all in a furious obstacle race together.

Luckily taxis are enormous—much bigger than one expects, and though my car is old and square and taxi-shaped, it is much smaller than they are, reassuringly smaller, for it gives me several useful inches to spare each side in our alarming game of follow-my-leader through the traffic.

But what is quite unfair, an advantage which taxis use quite unscrupulously, is their power of turning. They can turn, so it seems to me enviously watching them, in not much more than their own length. They can twist and dodge, and park in places I could never hope to get into. It is most unfair. Down we all rush into one of the narrow streets we frequent, and there, blocking the way completely, is an enormous van unloading its entrails into the back door of a shop in the most leisurely infuriating fashion. Clearly it will be there for half-an-hour at least. But are the taxis infuriated? Do they glare at their watches in a frenzy as I do, late already? Not at all. They take one glance (not at their watches, but at the width of the street), they spin round their steering-wheels, they turn completely and face about with no effort at all, and off they go back again the way they came to try another street. As for me, I must wait for the lorry, or wear myself out edging round backwards and forwards an inch at a time. A taxi is the only motor-car I would prefer to my own.

Today the traffic seems worse than ever; but then every week it seems worse than ever, as no doubt it is. And Peter is delighted: this sea of movement which surrounds us suits his hilarious mood: he is excited by the noise and the lights and the swirling crowds of people. For the first time in his life he feels that it might be fun to drive a car.

"But I think I'd like to practise somewhere else first," he tells me, considering the road ahead packed solid with cars like a box of uneven bricks. And while we wait our turn to move, I think how driving a car without collision in such a welter is a quite astonishing skill for us all to take for granted. And I think how many skills modern man learns as a matter of course: reading and writing and travelling about by trains and buses, using all kinds of machinery and gadgets, living in the complicated setting of a modern city. They are the ordinary things which every child learns without thinking. But what a waste that we must each of us learn them afresh, that they are lost when we die, and cannot be handed on like books or furniture. I have all kinds of minor skills which Peter and John might like when I go—knowing my way about London perhaps, or driving in traffic. One of them might fancy my bad but fluent French, or the skills we all learn by middle-age of talking easily to strangers, putting shy people at their ease, or smoothing over awkward social silences by what Henry James calls "spreading chatter thin." I can cook, and make clothes, and hang wall-paper on walls—a host of humdrum accomplishments—none of them of any great value, but still worth having if we could simply take them over without the bother of learning. But since I cannot share them out between the boys like coloured pencils, Peter will have to learn to drive a car himself.

"But I'd like to practise somewhere else first," he says, looking at the cars packed solid for as far as he can see. He looks at me and grins. "Somewhere where there's more room to wobble if I want to."

THE YEAR OF A HOUSEHOLD WITH SCHOOL-
children has a rhythm of its own as clearly-marked and
regular as the rhythm of a farmer's year. It begins at the end of
September with the children back to school after two months'
summer holiday, for autumn is the start of the year in a household as it is on a farm or at school, with new classes, new family
plans and all kinds of New Year household resolutions. It begins energetically with a hundred things to catch up with after
the holidays. This time we will organize our affairs (it is always
one of the resolutions), we will not let Christmas overtake us
unawares as it always has done other years. We will be ready,
we decide. But we never are: no housewife ever is. For between October and Christmas there is much less time than we
think. Autumn lingers late in the south of England, and it is
Christmas almost before the last leaves have fallen from the
plane-trees in the squares. It is always the same. We are never
ready. We felt we had plenty of time left still for planning and
shopping and finishing off a hundred odd things before the
holidays began again, but here it is already upon us, with the

shops full of gloves and handkerchiefs and all the trivia of Christmas, and John already discussing how much of the holiday he will spend in London and how much in the country. Almost before there is time to put away our summer clothes, the boys are taking their end-of-term exams, the morning post arrives later and later, and the holidays engulf the household with plans for parties and Christmas lectures and dancing-classes, with the boys and their friends restlessly in and out, and every meal a proper meal—no bread and cheese and cups of coffee.

Christmas lasts till almost the end of January, too long for me always, but never for the children. And the term which follows seems always to them the longest term of the year, dark and cold and full of minor ailments. But for me it is never too long—never long enough, for it is the one time of the housewife's year, as of the farmer's, when we can hope to have some time to ourselves and do the extra things we always intended. Most of the winter comes after Christmas, and Christmas to Easter seems always the longest, least broken stretch of the year. There is nothing much happening in the house, and it is too soon to care about spring-cleaning; there are no holidays or visitors or expeditions in this winter season. If any housewife plans some major undertaking in the household, or hopes to find some time for her own private life, now is her chance. For even though this winter calm is likely to be troubled by family ailments, by colds and temperatures and weeks of flu, with all the endless up-and-down muddle of meals on trays—even so, if the housewife cannot clear some space in her life between Christmas and Easter then she never will. For when once Easter comes, the year changes its pace to a faster more insistent rhythm which overrides our private plans. It is not only the month of the Easter holidays, but the summer term is a restless time, never properly settling down between days off and half-term, and summer exams which seem to start, like Christmas, long before they should. And in the summer months too, William's working routine which is so peaceful for the household, breaks up into a long disturbance of travel and visits and week-end meetings and holidays to be organized inbetween. And though as a working year it might seem that most of it was not work but holidays, that is because they are not holidays to the housewife, but extra work, since *she* is not on holiday at all, but running the hotel where the holidays are taken. The summer is the housewife's busiest season, and the house runs most easily when all the family are hard at work.

Every year I make ambitious plans of what I will do from Christmas to Easter. I will teach myself Spanish perhaps, or reorganize the house, or finish the second half of my garden book, which grew too long and had to stop in the middle as a separate volume. This year, so I tell myself always—when Christmas is over and the boys back at school—I will shut myself up and work till the spring. I will clear my time ruthlessly of family affairs, and train myself to ignore my household as if it had nothing to do with me. But I never can. There are too many meals to cook, too many people in and out of the house, and a doctor's telephone can never be ignored. Yet every winter I try. I shut myself up and neglect my friends and plan the meals with dishes which need the least cooking. It is a dismal time always, and irritable with the frustrations of work interrupted. For I never do more than a fraction of what I intended. The spring sun interrupts me always before I have finished, disturbs me like a hibernating animal restless and hungry in the first warm weather.

And now to-day is the first day of spring. Not spring by the calendar, which is always late, but by the weather. Yesterday was winter still, with the sky above the houses muffled in clouds and the walkers on the pavements muffled in coats. But suddenly this-morning the spring is here, the warm wind soft and fitful, the sky astonishingly high and clear, and everywhere a radiant brightness as if the air shone with invisible quicksilver. It is early March, almost a month before the official spring, and in the country this first soft weather finds only a landscape dry and derelict after the winter. No doubt beneath the dead leaves in hedge-bottoms there will be new green shoots if we look for them, the warmth will stir numb roots to life, tight buds will soon begin to swell. But this early spring is a disappointment always in the country, we long for the full blossoming, are impatient of this slow awakening to life.

In a city it is different. Spring comes earlier, as all the seasons do, for here they are man-made and we are restless always for change. In a town spring comes with the first warm day, and a single sunny morning in March will bring it to full flowering. For this urban spring has nothing to do with roots darkly stirring underground, there is no slow unfolding leaf by leaf, but a sudden heady excitement, gay and frivolous and artificial. It is as if the new season had been prepared somewhere else to be supplied to the town, waiting packed-up and ready in perfect condition, like flowers at Covent Garden, to spread in festival through the streets on the first sunny morning.

For city springs are seasons of the shops: they flower in new bright cottons for summer frocks, white gloves immaculate as daisies, and tiny gay straw hats absurd with flowers—frivolous stuff versions of primroses in country hedges, as fresh and as frail and as perishable. Yesterday was winter, but the shops will know that to-day is spring. And it is in shop-windows that daffodils first flower among the new bright shoes and scarves for summer. The earliest pink of almond-blossom against dark twigs is in West End windows, among pale cotton frocks as delicate and uncrushed as newly-opened flowers. Violets and snowdrops are heaped for us on trays at street corners, fragrance in warm intoxicating waves blows over us from yellow banks of mimosa on street-side barrows. For city spring is gathered flowers, the brightest and the earliest and the best, all brought in and arranged to deck the town for our delight.

Three Years of Growing

And since this first day of spring should always be festival, I shall leave the house and go shopping. Not to-day to buy shirts for the children, nor socks for William, nor new kitchen tea-cups, nor any of the dull household needs always waiting on my list, but to go round the shops for nothing at all but my own enjoyment. Perhaps I shall buy a new hat: perhaps not. For even the buying of hats is a practical business, and to-day I am out only for pleasure, to welcome the sun and greet the new season. I am out in celebration that the winter is over at last.

All down the road the windows are open. Tulips in window-boxes have blossomed overnight. Hall-porters stand in doorways and smile at the street—smile for no reason except that the air is warm with sunshine and the sky a milky radiance of blue.

I pass a man with a flower in his coat. Would he have worn it yesterday I wonder? or carried his hat in his hand as he does to-day? A girl goes by in a dress of the same pale yellow as the early butterflies which the first warm day draws out from winter hiding. Indeed all the young women I pass seem suddenly to be dressed in clothes newly-pale after the blacks and browns of winter, spring girls as bright as birds in the delicate fresh colours which blossom always in the first sunshine, lemon yellow and pale lavender and apple-blossom pink, flower-colours which fashion produces every year triumphantly at this same season, every spring as if for the very first time.

In the square at the bottom of the street the birds are singing, a thrush superbly, pigeons musically choking, and the fussy twittering of sparrows. The tracery of the plane-trees is thicker against the sky; there are buds on the almond tree, soon to open pink.

Oxford Street when I reach it is crowded as always, but to-day the slowly-surging people have a smiling holiday air, the relentless traffic seems milder and better-tempered. Above the roof of Marshall and Snelgrove's float coloured flags in celebration of the spring, and the cheerful white building looks even more than usual like a French casino. Scarlet buses glow in the sunshine, Jays on the corner have turned their windows to festival, Libertys pour out rivers of silks in clear spring-rainbow colours.

Do I need a white straw hat with tiny brown bows I wonder? or a pair of sky-blue shoes? Or a coat of buttercup-yellow linen? No. I need none of them, but that has nothing to do with my morning's intentions. I have not come out to shop, but because the sun is shining and the wind is warm: have come like everyone else to see blue shoes and yellow coats arranged like flowers in shop-windows, come to greet them as we greet the first swallows, because they mean the London spring is here. If I buy anything at all it will not be hats or coats or gloves or shoes, but a branch of golden mimosa to carry home and scent the house with warmth and summer.

Yet spring is a difficult season, too disturbing always, restless and dissatisfied like a yearly adolescence. We are unsettled when the west wind blows warm, curiously troubled by the clouds sailing over the blue patch of sky in the window. It becomes intolerable to stay indoors when every noise from outside is a siren-song to lure us from the house. But when we are out—what then? For the yellow coat is not what I want, nor even the yellow mimosa.

> *"In the Spring a young man's fancy lightly turns to*
> *thoughts of love."*

But then I am not a young man, and even when I was a young woman it was never quite so simple. For though one's love-affairs seemed all-engrossing, yet there still remained a wordless discontent at some profounder level. And perhaps the spring is an incurable illness always, and there is no help for our yearly discontent. Yet certainly we need some absolute pleasure, some violent delight which is complete, self-contained, reliable:

. 152 .

something we can swallow like a drug, knowing it will work, work every time without our trying. The happiness of our ordinary pleasures is too diffuse and fitful a quality to satisfy the urgent discontent of March—meeting friends or going into the country or reading poetry. In March these will not do. Our friends may be preoccupied, the wind blow cold off the bare hills, the poetry mock us with mere empty words.

"Nothing is so beautiful as spring."

Sometimes it is magic. Sometimes we listen and smile with delight. "When weeds in wheels shoot long and lovely and lush." Suddenly we are in some neglected orchard, with the sunlight filtered green on the yellow celandines and the first cow-parsley, and through the trees a thrush singing.

Certainly it is an intense enough pleasure, but not alas, not really reliable. "Nothing is so beautiful as spring." Sometimes it is simply a statement like any other—Nothing is so summery as linen. Nothing is so tiresome as the post-man late. Nothing is so beautiful as spring.

We sigh, and try something else. What we need is something as simple and reliable as switching on a light. And since through all the millions of years since it began, love-making has been arranged for us as an unfailing pleasure, then it really should be more complete and dependable than the chancy delights of Gerard Manley Hopkins or the sympathetic moods of our friends. So perhaps the young men are right, and there is nothing better than to follow their fancy in light love-affairs which blossom and vanish like daffodils.

I used to think when I was a child (for children are troubled by spring long before they are troubled by love), I used to think that the only thing would be to soar upwards into the sky, into the highest vault of blue and dive gloriously into a cloud. I dare say it might do: I dare say it is a fancy common to most children, since we all of us dream of flying, and no-one could gaze up into the spring sky without impatience of our earth-bound state.

Perhaps the violent delight of flying is what young men find in driving motor-cars fast. For when they rush about the roads at high speed it is not because they are in a hurry (indeed they seldom seem to be going anywhere in particular), but because they enjoy the rushing. We can still feel their exhilaration when they tell us about it afterwards. And they always *do* tell us: to boast of their speed to an audience later seems to be part of their pleasure. They went at 80 miles an hour they tell us, or 90 or 100 or whatever it is. And aren't they tremendous fine fellows? their voice seems to ask us, and aren't we no end impressed? If we are not, then it will doubtless be 200 miles the next time they tell us, for they are determined to win against our indifference, pushing up the miles like bids at an auction-sale.

To please them I will listen to whatever they like to tell me— 300 miles if they like—I will even be impressed if it will please them: anything so long as they do not expect me to go with them to be shown. For the days are long since over when I enjoyed rushing round the roads like a race-track with young men in motor-cars simply for fun. Listening to them now I am only reminded of how the children used to boast in just the same way about staying up late at night. Till midnight, they would say in portentous voices, and if I did not react with suitable horror, then the time grew later and later—one o'clock, two, three, four—they would slash away the hours with reckless impatience, stimulated by my indifference.

Even now at eleven and twelve years old they have not quite lost their childish wonder of the night. The world of darkness is still strange they feel, and at some crisis in the night hours so they seem to think, their day-time world will be changed by a mysterious transformation. If only they stay up long enough they may find this secret hour, as elusive always as the foot of the rainbow. Then the familiar day-time house, with only the clocks later and them dull with sleep, will be suddenly changed they feel, to some dark realm of midnight full of wonders.

Or so they used to think, but they grow more reticent, more careful of seeming childish; and perhaps too, less hopeful of magic. For they have often stayed up late, it has become a holiday tradition that with the morning ahead to lie abed in, they should stay up one night for as long as they please. It seems churlish to deny them so simple a pleasure. Though I think it is no longer the significant adventure it used to be, and the holidays often go by without them insisting on their staying-up rights. But in the spring they too grow restless for strange pleasures, and in the Easter holidays there is always a night when they stay up long after the household has gone to bed. It seems to have taken the place of their old Roof Riding, a game they gave up long ago of their own accord as really too childish.

These midnight sessions are most carefully planned. They agree beforehand which night it shall be, and make the most extensive preparations, collecting packs of cards and draughts and chess-men, saving their sweet allowance, storing-up cakes from tea, asking me for money so that they can buy themselves "something for supper." The night hours, they seem to feel, are hungry hours. Perhaps this is the point of the midnight feasts which all children seem to find so irresistible. Though for that matter most of our social occasions are arranged round meals, even the most unlikely ceremonies like weddings and funerals.

Certainly John and Peter do not intend to be hungry. They made out a list before they went to the shops, dull things like bread half-heartedly scribbled down, sausage-rolls with more conviction, chocolate in a decided hand, *apples* underlined, and LEMONADE POWDER triumphantly in large block capitals. They spent the morning shopping in the High Street with our largest basket, and now all this varied provender is collected together as

seriously and methodically as if for a siege, and they check it
against their list, reassuring each other that there really *is* enough
to see them through. They have arranged it in two piles, one each
end of the table, and they now consider it with the greatest satisfaction.

"Do you mind if I stay up till my usual time?" I feel I must
make sure I am welcome, since they have so clearly taken
possession of the evening.

"Dear Dardy. Of course. Stay as long as ever you like." They
are very lordly now that the whole night is theirs to dispose of.

"My dear, when you're hungry you can have some of our
food." John calls me "my dear" now with the exactly right in-
flection of patronizing affection. "My dear," he says, "you
haven't got any pudding," concerned at my empty plate, astonished that anyone should choose to miss this most important
part of John's meal.

They have settled down now for the night, have arranged
their chairs with two cushions each, and sit one each side of the
table within reach of the food at either end. Chess, they decide, is
what they will begin with, so they lay out the board between
them and begin their evening in earnest.

"Have a chocolate biscuit."

"Thanks. The apples look jolly good too. Have one?"

Every move they make on the chess-board is the signal to
offer each other something to eat, for they seem to regard this
as a social function demanding party manners and not their
usual help-themself methods.

I notice that the game of chess goes on surprisingly fast, and I
wonder what it is they really are playing. I watch them curiously, but they seem to move the pieces in the peculiar patterns
which I can recognize but have never mastered, so perhaps it is
chess after all, though not surely of a very advanced standard,
for they play as fast as dominoes.

I suppose I ought to go to bed and leave them, and it is a form of eavesdropping to stay and watch, but they seem not to care either way, so I settle down with my book.

They are discussing school as they play, though I am sure the best chess-players concentrate more on their game.

"Greek's a silly language," Peter pronounces scornfully. "They never say anything except things like 'We are great through our arts,' or 'He possesses honour on account of his virtue.' It's always the most awful bag-wash. Never anything you'd ever want to say like 'What are we having for tea?' or 'Need I have a bath?' "

"Well, Latin's just as bad." John is mildly defiant since he has not started Greek. "I don't see how they ever *talked* in Latin."

I could never see either, but then my Latin was never of a very high standard, scarcely better than theirs is now, though they still come to me hopefully for help with their homework. But what Latin I ever had is too faint and far-off now to see clearly, and if I remember at all it is mostly chance. If they ask me a word and what does it mean? I can never remember. Even if I ever knew, it has receded now so far to the back of my memory that the telescope of my consciousness can no longer find it. The meanings float vaguely about in the dim pool at the bottom of my mind, and only if the children bring me their book and I read it through quickly without trying, then the words may draw up the meanings like hidden fish from the pool, and sometimes I can catch them by surprise before they escape again. But it is no use applying myself. Like a dim star which disappears if we gaze at it intently, I must look away a little, and catch my Latin sideways from the corner of my eye.

They have left dull things like Greek and Latin now, and John is talking for his own amusement. "He made a bee-line for the door. But why a *bee*-line? Why not a *wasp*-line?" Peter only grunts an answer, and John plays with his new fancy. "He made a fly-line for his gun. I made a butterfly-line for the sugar."

"O shut up." Peter is impatient. "Don't waffle. I hope you know, my dear good brother, that all this time you've been waffling away I've been waiting for you to move?"

Waffle and bag-wash—how odd it is that slang always sounds so old-fashioned. Even when it is new it already has the air of a period piece. But John cares nothing for Peter's impatience, and goes on airily.

"And there was an old woman walking along the pavement, very small and tidy, with her head absolutely *buried* in an enormous white hat."

They have finished their game of chess and pushed the board to the end of the table, where the pile of food is reduced now to the duller things like sausage-rolls. They have started a card-game—whist it looks like, but *can* they play whist with only two people? But then I remember one holiday when I went to the station to meet John coming home from a visit to friends. And seeing no small familiar figure among the crowd on the platform I searched the train and found him at last, soundly asleep through all the noise and bustle of arriving. He was comfortably settled in a corner of the carriage, his head pillowed on the rucksack which he always takes for luggage, and spread out on the seat beside him a complicated game of cards.

"I was playing pontoon," he said, waking up with a beaming smile of welcome. "I've been playing pontoon with myself for *hundreds* of miles. But the bother *is*, I keep on cheating myself because it's such fun to cheat and it doesn't matter. But then it spoils the game you see, because if you cheat all the time it doesn't really count when you win."

Whist for two is simple I should think, after cheating pontoon for one, and certainly they not only play but talk to each other as well.

JOHN: I've got your birthday present. Can you guess what it is?

PETER: No. Tell me.
JOHN: It's something you want. You'll be jolly pleased.
PETER: Go on. *Tell* me. I can't guess.
JOHN: It's a book of five-figure log tables.

He announces this extraordinary present with perfect confidence, and clearly he is right, for Peter is genuinely delighted.
"I *say*. Jolly d. It's *exactly* what I want. Thanks *awfully*."

John beams with satisfaction, for giving presents is a pleasure
he can never resist. When he was little he would come to me
crying bitterly because he had given away his favourite toy and
wanted it back.

"And it's easy to pack," Peter goes on, still thinking of his log-
tables. "And of all the housework I do—" (he pauses to take a
trick, and I wait in astonishment for what he will say next)
"what I hate doing most of all is packing up Christmas presents."

Well I never. And how like his father. For at Christmas
William is always gloomy, and comes in from the hospitals
complaining how he has had to creep into the wards through
holly and tinsel and great expanses of cotton-wool snow, and
catch his patients as best he can between carol-singing and
Christmas dinner.

Peter goes on thoughtfully. "I don't like packing things for
summer holidays either—I don't like *any* sort of getting things
ready."

Just what he supposes he does in the way of organizing I cannot imagine, and I consider gloomily how much organizing *I*
have to do for us all, and always shall have to do I suppose, to
keep the household running. There are times, especially in the
summer holidays, when my one wry comfort is that there will
be one occasion at least which no-one can expect me to arrange,
and that is my own funeral. Then, if never before, it will all be
done for me: someone else quite certainly will have to be responsible.

"I *must* go to the barber's tomorrow and get my hair cut," Peter announces. "Even *I* think I must now. I don't take any notice when people keep saying I look like a girl, but when it's so long that it gets in my mouth instead of only in my eyes, then I think I'll have some cut off."

I never send them to the barber, however long their hair, for I think men cut their hair too short, and look far more distinguished when they let it grow over their ears.

"What I *hate* at the barber's," says John, "is when he sweeps my neck with a brush."

"I don't mind *that,* but I hate the clippers."

"I *love* the electric ones," John has always been a sensualist. "They make a lovely warm feeling in your neck and down your back and out at your arms and legs, and your head feels all bubbly."

I remember how I once found John sitting in a hot bath eating ice-cream, and on his face an expression of dreamy withdrawal as if he were listening to something I could not hear.

"I thought it might be a special new feeling you know, and specially nice," he explained to me. "But it isn't. The ice-cream's better by itself."

It is late now, long after midnight, though John and Peter seem as fresh as ever. But I am tired—cat-and-dog-tired as John calls it, but too warm and comfortable to rouse myself and go to bed. In the pauses of quiet when the boys are engrossed with their game or their eating I drowse off to sleep, a fitful sleep interrupted by snatches of talk.

"Mr. Smith showed me his butterfly-collection to-day," Peter is telling John. "He's got some jolly good ones, but they're all set in such an awful old-fashioned way—you know—their wings bent back and their feelers drooping down as if they were tired. It makes them look so *depressed,* poor things. I've reset all mine in the new way with their wings held up high so that they look awake and cheerful."

Three Years of Growing

I had no idea there were fashions in setting butterflies, but Peter is full of fascinating information. "Mr. Smith told me there're beavers in Europe. Did you know? On the old River Rhône there are. But they're *degenerate* beavers, so he says. What do you think beavers *do* when they're degenerate?" Peter pauses to consider this, but John has no ideas. "They can't very well get drunk, or stay in bed all day, or YOU KNOW WHAT." (This last in a melodramatic whisper.) "Mr. Smith thinks they don't build dams, but that's only lazy. It *must* be something worse. I'd like to meet a degenerate beaver."

But John is not interested in beavers, virtuous or otherwise, and does not answer. Or if he does I am too drowsy to hear, for his next question has nothing to do with anything.

"I never *did* like the Children's Newspaper, did you? Not enough nice juicy murders, and that sort of thing."

But I am almost too sleepy to listen. I think enviously of all the hundreds of people already settled in bed for the night—hundreds and thousands and millions of people, settled and comfortable in millions of beds for miles around me. I can just hear the boys talking a long way off about next term's cricket, a knowledgeable discussion about different boys' chances for the first eleven, and no sign of amazement any longer that when two boys are batting they must stand at different ends.

Will I come to the school cricket match of Boys versus Fathers? they want to know, waking me up. Yes I will, I tell them, for cricket is the only game I like to watch. Winter sports are too cold, and of warm-weather games, tennis is altogether too energetic and too cramped for comfortable watching. Cricket is the thing for the summer, with its wide lawn of a field, and open sky, and long sunny daylight and strawberries for tea in the cricket pavilion.

Besides, pavilion tea has its own entertainments, quite apart from the fathers in cricket caps and the excellence of the food provided by the head-master's wife. For as parents we only exist through our children, and in the hierarchy of the school world we take our rank from theirs. If they are new boys in the bottom class, then so are we. We must be humble and wait our turn, almost we must not speak unless we are spoken to by senior parents. As middle-of-the-schoolers we have learned our place and privileges, we are comfortably at home; but when our children reach the top class, then we are in the top class with them: we are grand and lordly, we benignly condescend. We are seniors soon to retire, already a little remote from the small-scale day-to-day politics of the world we are leaving.

Whatever Peter and John may feel, eager always for the next move forward in their growing-up, I shall be sorry to leave my Prep school. I shall miss my cricket-matches and pavilion teas.

For a moment I drift off to sleep, then back to the consciousness of my chair by the fire and the boys at the table. I must go to bed, I tell myself, but too drowsily for action. It is stupid to fall asleep here, dreaming of summer and cricket and somewhere a long time ago, in the shadow of high trees, with a butler walking across the grass towards us with frosted glasses on a tray. When was it I wonder? There were young men all about, I remember —sprawling in deckchairs or standing up tall and magnificent. And I was young too—in a green dress, with my arms very brown. And when a bat hit the ball the sound reached us twice over, in a faint following echo from the wall of the pavilion opposite—a hollow "plop"—like the sound of shelling peas when we press the round hollow end of the pod until it bursts open—a summery sound, and the children sitting in the sun— very small still—sitting side by side on the lawn shelling peas into a deep blue bowl. "Podding peas" they called it—and "podding strawberries"—their faces smudged with the juice and the lawn needing cutting—grown high with daisies—and the turtle-doves crooning in the meadow—and a river—(why is there always a river when I dream of summer?)—the water rippling clear under the dipping willow branches and the water-reeds swaying in the shallow current. And now this year too has turned down the green lane that leads to summer, with the sunlight in shifting dapples through the leaves. And there are kingcups flowering already perhaps in the watery places on the edge of the river, and the air very clear after rain—

"Dardy will be horrified if she hears you say that."

I wake up at my name as dogs do if we talk of them when they are asleep.

"What will I be horrified at?" But they will not tell me, they only grin; and since I am awake I really shall go off to bed now and leave them. For although the hour is most depressingly late, they are both as wide-awake and enthusiastic as when they started.

"We're not coming for *ages* yet," they assure me. "We're going to stay up *really* late this time, and see what happens."

What do they think will happen? I wonder, going upstairs. What is it they are so curious to discover in the dark night interval between one day and the next? But even if they knew they are too old now to tell me. "O, we talked about all sorts of things," they will say if I ask them in the morning. And wakened by the cold of getting undressed, I lie in bed waiting for sleep, thinking that as they grow older there is more and more of their lives that children no longer share with their parents. As if their minds were countries which meet us at a common frontier, but which grow and develop on the furthest side away from us, where we cannot reach them. If they are ever to grow up it must be like that, for their boundary with us is fixed and static, it is only at the far borders of their territory that they have the space and freedom they need to develop.

We have our shared frontier still: we meet to exchange greetings and information; but most of their life is private now, they do not tell us. Sometimes they bring casual reports of what they are doing in their autonymous kingdom; sometimes scraps of news reach us of the fresh lands they have found and conquered;

and sometimes rumours filter through of dark adventures we never suspected, like John's encounters with strange men.

For they are exploring fast, pushing out into new realms of knowledge and experience, and soon the main extent of their minds will be for us an unknown hinterland which we can only learn by inference or invitation, and not by the common right of travel. If we pry and insist then they will close their frontiers with us, hide away from our criticism the tentative and only half-understood activities of their new kingdom, withdraw to the furthest boundaries and push them out deliberately into the unknown away from our interference.

Whatever we do, much must always be for us unknown, for they are exploring not only their own minds which are much like ours, but also their own new world which is different. The life they will have to live is a generation away from ours, with new knowledge, different sympathies and ways of living. There is a war between their childhood and ours, science and social revolution. It is as if mankind, advancing in time, were advancing across an unexplored continent generation by generation. We who are adults now have occupied and developed our own stretch of country; but they, the next generation, must go further on into the next stretch. And how they should live in this new land we cannot tell them, for we do not know. We can show them how we have arranged our own country, many of their trees and flowers will be the same as ours, there are not so many different ways of enjoying the sunshine. Some of the enemies they meet will be the ones we have already come to terms with, primeval wolves which range all human boundaries, the unchanging despairs of our mortal condition.

Yet still their new country is not the one we know. There will be new problems which they will find the answer for better than we can, judging always in terms of our own past. And as they push their boundaries forward and further away from us, we must let them alone unless they invite us. I think they are not anxious to leave us unless we drive them away by petty authority and prying interference. If we stay in our own country, incurious but always friendly, perhaps they will live next door to us without irritation, will come to visit us backwards and forwards, finding their own way through the frontiers between the generations.

PART THREE

NOW
WE
LIVE
IN
LONDON

IT IS MORE THAN SIX YEARS NOW SINCE WE
came to London, long enough for us all to feel thoroughly at
home in the town, to grow roots like the vine I planted in a tub
in the yard the first year we came. It has grown now to an exuberant tree, so large that even when I pile all the telephone di-
rectories on a chair and balance myself on the top, I can no
longer tie on the highest branches to their supporting wires. It
pushes out every summer in vigorous new shoots across the
kitchen windows, and unless we like to eat our meals in a leafy
green shade like a woodland picnic, I can see that I shall have to
harden my heart and chop it down.

We have lived here long enough too for the house to need redecorating. The white paint has turned to primrose yellow as
white paint does, our favourite easy chairs need recovering,
there are dark smudges all the way up the staircase wall where
the boys have been up and down more thousands of times than I
like to reckon. The house now is like an old coat that we wear
every day and which has changed to the shape of our wearing,
bulging at the pockets, dragging on the buttonhole we fasten

most often, the sleeves frayed and baggy at the elbows; so that it is no longer an impersonal garment with its own separate sartorial shape, but a loosely-fitting skin which belongs to us and no-one else.

In the old clothes of people we know well—clothes hitched carelessly over a hook or flung across a chair—in these loose discarded coverings we still feel the familiar presence of the wearer, a faint lifeless echo of their shape and movements, like the presence of a snake which haunts its discarded skin. We know our friends' clothes as we know our friends' voices: there is no need to see them together.

So too this house has worn to the shape of the family life it has sheltered these six years of growing. It is shabby with too much use and needs redecorating, as we need a new suit of clothes for the spring. It is a milestone in the occupation of any house, and this second redecorating is no longer simply a choice of colours and curtains to suit our own personal tastes, no longer as if we were buying new clothes without knowing, except by hearsay, the life we should wear them for. This second redecorating of the house we live in is a collaboration between us and the house itself. The occupations which habit has settled in the different rooms will decide the new curtains as much as our own taste will. What new colour we paint the walls will depend now not simply on what colour we happen to fancy, but on whether we use the room most by day or by night, whether the wall shows marks at the door, and how much the carpet has faded. The house and our family life have grown together.

Nor is it only in the house that we feel at home after six years in London. We are all at ease now against our metropolitan background, and it is not only William who feels he belongs. The boys have moved on to their final school, have settled in from the start with the greatest satisfaction in their new school world, as if they had at last been admitted to a most desirable society which they had long been waiting to join. About their school-days now there is an easy man-about-town air which they find quite exactly to their liking. They treat their school as a club. There are rules of course, and the lectures must be attended; but apart from the lessons there are a hundred things going on for their amusement, there is a general atmosphere of tolerant goodwill, and the club-house is old and hospitable and conveniently in the centre of the town.

Among the members of this school-club there is plenty of choice for friends and companions. Certainly Peter and John are still among the lowest and least privileged of creatures: as new-boys and fags they are liable to all kinds of tiresome duties; but they appear not to mind. What matters, so they seem to feel, is that they now indisputably belong, that they are already safely established in the ranks of this congenial community, and that they too in time will enjoy the lordly privileged state of the senior members.

"O, *we* have no say. *We're* only new-boys—not fit to talk to," they tell me with a grin. "You can't expect them to notice *us*. We're just a lot of tiresome little tiddlers that they can't tell apart." So they announce with what seems to me the greatest satisfaction.

Indeed they are both most reassuringly satisfied at the moment with all their affairs, as if in these last years they had swallowed down and digested an enormous meal of new experience, and were now sitting back well-fed and at their ease in a comfortable consciousness of mastery of the world they live in. Physically they are both growing large and powerful, and for boys especially I suppose that gives a reassuring sense of confidence. Then too they have reached in their growing-up a peaceful interval of settled fair weather between the exhausting development from young children to boys, and the no doubt far stormier change which lies ahead in their adolescence before they become young men. But just now we all enjoy the sunshiny calm of this untroubled stage of their childhood. They are delightful companions, intellectually active and self-confident, but emotionally dormant, as if they were no more conscious of any emotional life than they are of their excellent digestions. Both processes seem to work perfectly well, with no attention from their owners.

Like William and the children, though less irretrievably, I too now feel myself to be a Londoner at last. I come back to the town now as one comes back home, with relief and affection and a sense of belonging. The strangeness of the surrounding city is no more disquieting now than the strangeness of unfamiliar country beyond one's village. The streets about our house are friendly and comfortable: this is where I live and I am glad now to be back. Coming into London again after the country I seldom now suffer the old dismay which once engulfed me; my spirits rise now, as William's I know always have done. We breathe in, with the very air of the city, a sense of expectation and excitement. We feel we are back where things are happening, where life goes on at a stimulatingly faster pace, so that we think faster, move faster, feel our steady country pulses quicken to the eager rhythm of city dwellers—a liveliness which bewilders those not used to it as mere feverish hurry.

How could we possibly have stayed away so long? we wonder, coming back to the quick streets. Why were we not drawn back sooner by the sense of missing all that must have been going on without us?

Which proves nothing at all about the merits of town and country life, proves nothing except that we ourselves are townees when we feel that is how it is.

Certainly when I am in the country I never miss the town. Not at all. In the country London is completely unimportant. Quite simply it ceases to exist: is something I half-remember now and then as if in a book I had once read. But coming back I feel how shut-away and vegetable was my slow green existence out there in the fields, how less than alive. And back in the streets again I smile with pleasure, my spirits quickened and excited in the lively city air. So I have turned into half a townee I suppose, as I once hoped I might do. And if this is what I hoped for, I was right, and it could not be more satisfactory, this double life in two separate worlds of town and country, each complete and absorbing.

Yet what is it we expect, coming back to London? Why are we excited? For there is no reason. Nothing is going to happen. We have only come back because school starts again next week and we must get ready. But in the air of big cities there is some unknown extra element which stimulates us. Even now, after years, I never step out into the street without a quick lifting of my spirits. I am only going to the shops to buy food for the family, or to the library to fetch a book, but always the street is a minor adventure, I look up and down expectantly from the doorstep.

There is another change too, that I often now notice the astonishing beauty of London, as I never did when we first came. For London is not a fine city as Paris is, nor even an English town like Oxford. It is seldom admirable in its material brick and stone, but as a picture, like the city scenes Utrillo paints, the lovely *blême* houses which are inspired by a reality of shabby rows of brick with the paint peeling off (as paint always is peeling off in Paris).

So too, London's ugly buildings lose their material identity in the subtle shifting light of English skies, and merge to dreamlike pictures of delicate lines and understated shadows and planes set sideways to the silvery radiance. The vistas of streets dissolve in a soft bluish mist, buildings seen one against another are outlined, each less clearly, as they blur with distance. It is sad that we have had no painter to show it to us. For Whistler's river is not this— it is too romantically self-conscious—and as for Canaletto, he paints London as he paints Italy; his serene bright spaces show us more of his own spirit than they do of the London scene.

For it is not, certainly not, the town-planning nor the architecture which are London's beauty. It is the English weather. And not the summer sunshine, which reveals her ugliness too clearly, but the ambiguous light of our inbetween seasons. On winter evenings especially, when the lamps of the town and the still faintly-shining sky reveal the city scene in a strange double illumination, then London is magically transformed. Trafalgar Square in a December dusk is no longer an untidy hotch-potch of unrelated buildings, but a mysterious picture in greys, the half-seen half-suggested planes of the buildings strangely catching the light, the distances lost in the gathering darkness, the rigid plumes of the fountains shattering to ghostly white as they fall in spray. Overhead the grey sky is changed to an ethereal pale blue behind the dusky yellow of the lamps, and the black plane-trees make lavishly decorative filigree patterns against the pale buildings. And through this mysterious scene there is the movement of the traffic sliding and gleaming, the small dark figures of walkers, and against the faintly-shining sky the starlings flying over in fluttering changing flocks.

It is one of the scenes I remember when someone says suddenly "London. Do you like living in London? Do you *really* like it after the country?" I remember one evening especially, standing at the end of the Strand, looking across Trafalgar Square as the daylight faded and the starlings came in to roost—flying over high up, fanning out, scattering, then coming together again, sweeping over in wide arching curves, hesitating before they settled, separate groups crossing each other in restless patterns of dark shapes against the pearly sky. No swans or doves or peacocks are more romantic than these wild birds so strangely drawn to the noisy company of the London night.

Starlings are London's birds, as the plane is London's tree, wild birds which live in the town from their own free choice. Nor do they seek out the parks as we might expect they would: they are city-dwellers of the streets and buildings. The green spaces are there as decoration of the town, not to pretend they are country. And I too no longer walk in the parks for my reassurance, as I did when we first came to this world of bricks and pavements. I no longer fill every window-sill with plants in pots, all of us equally homesick for the country air. Now I only grow a favourite few for green decoration here and there where I can be bothered to water them. Nor do I look out at the sky now so constantly through the windows, as I used to for the comfort of seeing that the clouds over city chimneys are the same clouds exactly as over the open fields. The clouds and the parks are pleasures still, but so are the streets and the people and the fascinating landscape of roofs and chimneys through the children's bedroom windows. As for Peter and John, they can scarcely remember the life of the farm where they first grew up, and certainly they have no wish at all to go back. The country does well enough, they feel, for holidays in the summer, but not—quite *certainly* not—for living one's proper life. They are delighted with their present status of young Londoners at the beginning of their teens, strolling in from school very lordly now and self-assured, swinging their door-keys on the end of a chain, urbanely discussing together the snippets of town news. They have both grown tall and long-legged, and I watch them go off together down the street in the morning when I wait for the postman, very much townees in their new dark grey suits, their school-books hidden in a discrete attaché-case, over their arm a neatly-rolled umbrella—two tall figures indistinguishable from behind from any of the other dark-grey-suited young men along the pavement. In the autumn especially, when their suits are new, they look from behind quite astonishingly urbane. For school suits have their own individual life, I find, which lasts exactly a year. The new ones are measured and made in the summer holidays, and they must last until the end of the school year the next July. Clearly they must, for it would be useless to start a new suit at an inbetween season like May. It would never last through the year till the following spring, for the summer holidays are always a time of such outrageous growing that no

clothes which fit boys in May would ever go round them again
the next September.

Even with such precautions the first essential for any suit is
that it should start off far too large. Nothing can actually *fit* boys
of twelve and thirteen for more than a few months: there must
be a period before and after of too-large and too-small, and all
mothers come to regard as a kind of provident luxury, any room
to spare in jackets and trousers and shoes and socks. So off the
boys go to the tailor with fierce instructions that all sleeves must
reach to their knuckles, all trousers to the floor, that shoulders
must fit loose over all the layers of vests and jerseys and games
sweaters I dress them up in, despite the summer heat, especially
for the tailor to measure over. For I would far rather turn up
hems the first term than let them down the second; and as for
the third term, that is an ordeal we must all get through as best
we can—boys and me and suits together—with tactful patches
on elbows, strategic darns on trouser-seats, and the thinnest of
summer shirts under the jackets they must remember now not
to stretch in too heartily or they will certainly split across the
shoulders.

Yet even when their suits are at their newest, it is only from
behind that Peter and John could be mistaken for their elders.
When they turn round their faces betray them, still soft and
smooth and the bones scarcely showing, still fringed, when they
come in at tea-time, with the same untidy rat-tails of hair wet
from the shower when they changed after the river. For they
have given up cricket and football now, and they row on the
river instead. Nor is their still prodigious appetite for tea at all
what one would expect, but an enthusiasm altogether incongruous with such urbanity. Tea-time is still the time for news,
but it is reporting which has imperceptibly changed its character.
Their personal lives are more private now, and not to be revealed indiscriminately to parents. It is not that there are deliberate secrets, but the news of the day has been surveyed I feel,

and censored. Some incidents have been chosen for telling, and others passed over as not at all suitable for the family tea-table. They realize that in relationships between people who live closely together there must be a certain tact.

"Nothing's happened to-day. Nothing at all," John says reflectively, full enough of tea to be sociable, but too lazy to take the trouble to entertain us.

"You never tell us school news nowadays," I grumble, knowing quite well that it is unfair, but that he needs goading.

"Yes, I do," John responds indignantly. "I save up all sorts of things to tell you."

So he does, but I can never have enough reports from such a fascinatingly different world.

"Well, tell me for instance what you do in the mornings."

"Well." John settles down with a grin, for he always enjoys amusing us if we once encourage him to start. "Well, I never get up in time for breakfast, so I've given up breakfast. . . . But you know all about that. Then I grab everything and run, and if I'm not too late even to look at my watch, I time myself to the bus stop to see if I can break my all-time world record. And if I save an extra second I think 'Triumph. Lovely. To-morrow morning I can have an extra second in bed.' It takes most of the way on the bus to get my breath back, and when I've got it back it's time to watch and see if the traffic lights are red so's I can jump off at the corner and save at *least* ten yards' walk back to the school gate. And if the lights are green I jump off just the same. Then I rush across the yard and dive into the house and fling my things in a corner. Then I find my friends and thump them hard on the back to show how pleased I am to see them. Then *they* thump *me* harder still to show they're pleased to see me too. And we all rag and lark about and shout at the tops of our voices and the din's simply deafening. You'd *hate* it. Then the Head of the Common Room comes in and yells through his hands at us to shut up—and I don't wonder either, you've no *idea* how awful the din is. And after a bit we stop shouting at the tops of our voices and only shout at the bottom, but we keep on forgetting, and it keeps on getting louder again, and he keeps on screaming at us through his hands——" And so on, and so on, through a cheerful energetic deafening morning which makes me feel dazed even to imagine. It is a double account, half larky schoolboy enjoying the noise, half detached adult amused at the scene.

To-day however there is no need to invent the news for tea-time, for Peter has come home triumphant, standing proudly in the middle of the kitchen to make his announcement.

"This afternoon out rowing I broke an oar."

He says no more but stands confidently smiling, clearly waiting to accept our homage of surprise and admiration. But as a housewife it seems to me a very doubtful achievement to break an expensive thing like an oar. I should have thought the boat club would scold not praise, and tell him to be more careful next time. But John like Peter spends his games afternoons rowing boats up and down the Thames, and he therefore knows better.

"I *say*. *Jolly* good. Congratulations," and he slaps his brother on the back, beaming with approval. "Don't you see?" he explains to me condescendingly, "it means that Peter's so strong and rows so hard that no oar can take the strain."

"Yes," agrees Peter modestly, accepting such praise as no more than his due. "And they said did I want the pieces of oar to bring home as a keepsake?"

"And did you bring them?" I asked with misgiving, for the young men I used to know in the old days also had oars as keepsakes, not broken oars either, but whole ones because they had won races. And whole oars are so excessively long that the only place in a house with a wall big enough is the staircase. So that I always knew that if I married a young man with an oar, I should also be marrying a staircase with an oar on the wall for the rest of our lives.

But I need not worry about Peter. He is not single-minded enough for the true sportsman, and his games are kept very much in their proper place.

"No, I didn't have the pieces," he says. "I looked at them and I thought they were too big. My study's in enough mess already. I thought I wouldn't bring anything else to clutter it up any more than it is. What I *did* bring home," and he looks at me ruefully, no longer the triumphant oarsman with an admiring audience, but changed now to an apologetic member of the household asking favours of the housekeeper. "What I did bring home is my spare rowing change." His voice changes to a coaxing note and he smiles at me doubtfully. "Could you just wash them a bit before next week?"

As well he might be doubtful, for as he pulls out wet vest and shorts and socks the kitchen is suddenly filled with the peculiar pungent smell of river mud at low tide. It is a smell I have grown used to now. I know what it is. I no longer go sniffing round the house as I used to, suspicious of the drains.

"But I can't possibly get them clean," I grumble, discouraged by the stains of bilge-water and black oil, and patches of mould and fungus from being rolled up wet in a locker for weeks together. "I don't suppose I can even get the smell out, much less the dirt."

"Oh yes you can, dear Dardy." (I might have accepted with enthusiasm, so confident is Peter's tone now, so well he knows me.) "You'll do them *beautifully*. You always *do*." And he pats me gently on the back a few times to encourage me. "They're not meant to come white, you know. It's only that the bits between the stains are supposed to be a pale enough grey to look as if they started off white once upon a time." Peter grins. "Otherwise they think we let down the tone of the school on the tow-path."

No wonder they think so. The clothes Peter and John bring me home to wash would disgrace a chimney-sweep in his chimney, for I am sure no chimney-sweep smells like this, of mould, and wet, and rancid oil. But I have come almost to like the smell, for smells more than most things we judge by their associations, and for me this smell means rowing. I will put up with it, will wash and scrub and bleach their vests and shorts and socks, not willingly, but as the price I must pay for afternoons at the river, watching them row.

These river afternoons are a new extension of our London life, more fascinating far than the football and cricket fields of their other schools. For rowing, I have always noticed, creates a special atmosphere of its own, quite different from other games. It is the atmosphere of another club, a riverside club with the boat-house for home and the river as territory, and a general urbane air of the greatest ease and friendliness and goodwill. It is a community naturally democratic; naturally since only the best are admitted—a conviction never stated, nor even hinted, but which is somehow implicit in everything they do. Rowing is best. There is no arrogance about it, no need to boast. It is simply a fact of nature, that Rowing is Best.

So that all rowers are princes together in the most satisfactory way, and coming back to this atmosphere of democratic privilege I recognize the same young men I used to know in the old days. These new rowers are just as easy, just as lordly; their untidy hair and dirty shorts and muddy feet all shine for me just as thick with gold-dust now as they did then. They are not my own generation any longer, they are my sons now, not my young men, but it makes no difference to my pleasure in their world observed. When I went to watch them in the old days it was not the young men's relationship to me which drew me, but their princely confidence in this different delightful world, so remote from the poor grey streets of the industrial city where I grew up that I saw it always half from the outside, as a dazzlingly romantic life where I too was free and accepted simply by going with my companions as their audience.

It is what I am now, an unofficial audience; there is no change at all either in them rowing or in me looking on. I watch my sons and their companions as I watched my young men and theirs. They are just as lordly and I am just as delighted. But as an audience I was then, and I am now, almost completely unsatisfactory. For I do not care in the least who wins. I have never been able to care. It is not a question of losing cheerfully or winning modestly, or any of the other sportsmanlike virtues which moralists believe to be encouraged by playing games. In me they need no encouragement at all; they flourish like weeds. What matters for me is that rowing is one of the pleasant worlds which are only created by the truly privileged, a river-world of leisure and lordliness and a youthful flowering of health and high spirits. It is a community with most seriously-considered values which are yet of a perfect irresponsibility, and that I suppose could be one of the definitions of privilege.

Certainly I can see that if young men are to row boats on rivers for exercise, then the obvious thing is to row them fast. And if there are several boats, then clearly they will all try to row faster than each other. That I can see. But so long as they all row at near enough the same speed to keep up the competition, that seems to me all that matters. But there. It only proves my inadequacy. And I have always done my best. I have tried, to begin with, to tell which boat is which, for I can see that is something I must know as a fundamental principle. But even this elementary distinction I find almost impossible, so much alike they all look, and so like the middle distance of a Canaletto painting of a regatta, with the regular rows of parallel oars and tiny white blobs of rowers in the narrow painted boats. It is much more real as a picture than a race, but I can see that if I am to follow at all I *must* know which is which, and I try again. Yet even when they help me—some enthusiastic young man in the old days, some enthusiastic boy now, someone who points out the boat I must watch, and explains that the oars I must cheer for are blue

or pink or green or whatever it is, so that even I can recognize
the flash of colour as the blades turn rhythmically over the water
—even when I do know which side I am on, even then what
seems important is that the scene should move and compose in a
satisfying pattern, that the light should fall just so on the shining
water, that the trees should fling and toss in the wind, tossing
and flinging my spirits with them till I too shout and cheer as the
boats go by, wild and drunk with sudden excitement.

But the one essential question—whether one boat rather than
another will be first to pass a certain point—that, I humbly accept, I shall never be able to care about. It is just as well that
Peter and John never read anything I write, and will not realize
that I never know whether they have won or lost until they tell
me: that if I smile to greet them off the river it is simply my usual
smile of affection, and if it seems to them sometimes a pleased
smile of triumph, and sometimes a rueful smile of sympathy, that
is simply because they interpret it to suit themselves, as my
young men no doubt did too, coming to be admired exactly as
the boys do now, and me just as pleased to see them.

It is for other reasons than winning races that I enjoy my river
afternoons. I like to stand about the tow-path with the river open
in front of me, wide here and serene, winding in great level
loops under its bridges and out of sight, a placid tolerant river
with room for everyone. I like it best at high tide, brimming to a
silver sheet of water almost at eye-level, washing against the
concrete ramp in regular slapping waves as bigger boats go by.
Sometimes in the high tides of spring and autumn it floods the
road and turns the boat-house to a Noah's Ark island, changing
an ordinary schoolday afternoon to holiday adventure. But the
river is always beautiful, whether the sun shines on blue water,
or the mist drifts in with the tide and smudges the distance,
whether the trees on the opposite bank are leafy or bare or half-
dissolved and insubstantial in the silvery light. There are summer
afternoons so brilliant that we screw our eyes to slits against the

dazzle, and mysterious winter evenings when the dusk obliterates the surface between air and water so that ghostly half-seen boats seem to float in space. The river is always enchanted, and the banks are part of its different world, lit by shifting upward reflections from the shining water, like the light from the sea. And the light, as always near water, has a curiously penetrating, irradiating quality, as if it were a solvent which dissolved all solid objects and shrunk their outlines. So that the buildings along the bank, and the people on the tow-path, and the boys balanced in their flimsy boats are all of them isolated and small and separately scattered upon this fluid scene of sky and light and water.

Sometimes I am taken up on to the balcony of the boat-house, but the balcony is the royal box reserved for the rowing aristocracy, and parents I feel, must wait to be invited. And the boat-house balcony, like all balconies, has the curious effect of turning those who stand on it to royalty. On the ground we are all alike, we are reasonably modest unself-conscious people. But once put us up on a balcony and we change at once to royal creatures who graciously acknowledge the salutations of our inferiors below. We stand up straighter, we compose our faces, we hold our heads high and smile benignly, lifting our hand a little perhaps, in salute and blessing. Kings after all are not the wise or the clever or the strong or the just: kings are simply the ones who appear on balconies. It is very reassuring, and very good for our self-esteem. It is why dictators should never be allowed on balconies, for it is too easy—no more than a dozen wooden steps to climb, and there we are translated.

When once we are over the irresistible impulse of bowing to those below us, the boat-house balcony has tea to offer, tea most powerfully strong, of a dark and leathery tan, as games tea always is. It is the right and proper drink for afternoons in the open air, as champagne is for weddings. And though I like my tea as pale as straw, I would not have this brew even a shade less mahogany, swallowing it down, not as tea at all, but as a special

. 183 .

boat-house beer. And would I like some more? a near-by boy will ask me with most courtly concern for my comfort. For their manners to visiting parents are irreproachable always, though whether they can really like us there I have never been able to decide, for this is a club so very urbane that there is no way of telling.

I lean on the wide wooden rail of the balcony and look across the river. A voice at my side is explaining how they build boats by hand. Further along someone is wondering whether ten people can travel comfortably to Henley all in one motor-car. But even I could tell them the answer to that. Ten people can. I used to be one of the ten and it is the best of all kinds of travel.

Beyond the voices the sounds of the river come echoing over the water, further off there is a murmur of traffic, and beyond that the distant hum of the town: receding layers of sound one behind the other, which are suddenly shattered by a burst of furious cheering from the boys at the other end of the balcony. Two boats go past along the river, two rigid eight-legged water-insects hurrying by, almost level with each other as they pass below us. The boat I must shout for is winning, they tell me, as soon as they can make me hear through the cheering. But that is another difficulty about rowing: even when I have made out which boat is which, and decided that this time I really will keep my mind on the race and cheer as I should, even then, unless there is a really serious gap between them, I can seldom tell which boat is in front of the other. The perspectives of rivers which wind as the Thames does are altogether too difficult to understand, and I shall give up trying.

The boat-house behind us is filling up with hungry boys, some of them still tousled and in shorts, some of them changed neatly back into school suits, their hair still wet from the shower, combed down flat and self-conscious as if for a party. But even at their tea-time tidiest they look casual and unkempt beside the pictures of Victorian rowers which decorate the boat-house walls. These astonishing creatures survey us from their faded photographs most carefully composed in drawing-room groups. They are immaculately dressed as Victorian gentlemen with watch-chains, and kid gloves, and top-hats held negligently in their hands. Brought in specially for them to pose round is a most unlikely-looking drawing-room table. One rests a hand on it, another his gloves, another sets down his top-hat just where we expect an aspidistra. They are all very serious and responsible and no-one smiles. But did these tailors' dummies really go rowing on the river? Did they too come in wet and tousled and smelling of mud? I suppose they must have done. I look at them again, mentally changing their gloves and top-hats for rowing vests and shorts—but no, long trousers I suppose it would be—not shorts in that prudish age. But what I cannot get over is their hair— hair set deliberately in waves and quiffs, hair combed elaborately sideways or forwards, most carefully arranged in fringes and love-locks, and what John calls side-burns. They look the most surprising bounders.

We knew of course that this was the fashion for mid-Victorian *men:* these are the hair-styles we have seen in hundreds of Victorian protraits. But somehow I never thought of *boys* with their hair so carefully arranged, certainly not boys just back from rowing on the river. They look scarcely respectable: they look as if they might forge cheques. And all because of our modern convention that men must not consciously arrange their hair. They must cut it off short and brush it back straight without thinking. They must be gruff and manly and unconcerned about their appearance. But how odd really, when man was born the peacock.

The boat-house now is full to bursting, its wooden structure clattering and echoing to thumps of feet and boats and lurching bodies. Boys stroll out from the boat-shed beneath us, large and easy, awkward and relaxed at the same time, like the half-grown puppies of very large dogs. They fold their arms and loll against

. 185 .

the door-post, fling off sweaters, exchange laconic remarks, sling their sweaters round their shoulders with the sleeves tied round their necks, and wander in and out grotesquely foreshortened as they pass below us. From time to time groups come together and carry a boat down the ramp and into the river, walking into the water unconcernedly in their shoes and socks like a team of amphibious godlings, too proud even to notice that the river is up to their knees. Nothing could possibly be more princely, nor more destructive for the socks they bring me home to wash. I can see quite well why the kitchen smells of river mud when the boys unpack their rowing clothes, why it is the background smell of our tea-time news, especially at the end of term, when everything at once comes home to wash and the kitchen has the air of a very disreputable jumble-sale. To-day at tea John came in beaming with satisfaction, bringing us a story like a bag of sweets to hand round the tea-table.

"In front of me in the bus a little boy was sitting with his mother. And all at once he got very excited and bounced up and down, and said 'Look. Look. That's the sort of car I want when I'm grown-up. That's the one I told you about and you didn't know—that nice big black one with flowers all over.' And do you know what it was when I looked out to see?" John asks us, savouring his story. "It was a *hearse in a funeral.*"

As John realizes, this is unexpectedly fine treasure. We seldom come on anything so perfectly suited to the tea-table without the least elaboration. And to-day Peter is ready to amuse us too, for he has left far behind him now the serious small boy who considered the bewildering world with such anxious and unsmiling attention.

"I got caught to-day for skipping the art class," he tells us. "To-day was Practical Art and I can't stand it. Practical Art means drawing your own pictures, and I can't possibly draw anything except science experiments, so I skip it whenever I can. But sometimes they catch me and I have to go, so I've worked out a special picture and I do it every time. It's the corner of a barn with beams everywhere. That's not so bad, because it's all straight lines and angles and I can do it with a set-square and ruler. And when I've done it once I do it all over again on a different scale, and I use my slide-rule to work it out."

Both Peter and John find this so irresistibly funny that they collapse on the table in giggles, and it is some time before Peter can go on.

"Sometimes the Art master comes round and asks what it is, and I say 'It's a barn,' and he says 'Humph. Needs some sacks about' and he scribbles in some floppy-looking sacks—but *I* never draw sacks because they're not straight lines." Peter stops to eat a large slice of cake before he goes on. "My only other picture is a view through a window into a yard with a wall round it. I do it sometimes as a change from barns. At the end of the yard there's the next-door house with a television aerial. That's all straight lines too, but it's harder still to tell what it is. It looks exactly like a cat's cradle."

"You could do a rainbow over the roof with your compasses," John suggests.

"Yes. I thought of that. And rain too, with a ruler. And, oh yes, that reminds me. I've found something to do in London the next Sunday it rains. We can go to the Science Museum and learn some new swear-words."

This seems an unlikely education for a museum to offer but Peter explains.

"They've got a lovely new machine a boy told me about the other day. The only bother is it's so popular you have to wait in a queue to have a turn with it. It's a tape-recorder, and you say things quietly into it at one end, and then after a bit it says them back at the other end, but *full-blast* through a loud-speaker. And there's just enough time inbetween for you to escape before anyone can catch you, so everyone says the worst swear-words they know into it, then run like the wind before they come shouting out on the loud-speaker. There's always a crowd listening, and almost most fun of all is seeing how cross the assistants get when they can't find who said it."

"Gorgeous," says John. "We can go with William and Dardy in the car to the Victoria and Albert (they're sure to go you know—they always spend their time looking at pictures and things when it rains). Then we can leave them and go to the swearing-machine."

I can see that this is unexpectedly good entertainment for a wet Sunday afternoon, and I wonder if I could go too, and leave the "pictures and things." For I often go with them to the Science Museum, a holiday attraction which has supplanted the Natural History Museum in Peter's affections. Nor does he any longer call it the Skee Muss as he used to—a childish affectation long since discarded. And just as he used to explain to me the evolution of birds, he now explains the scientific demonstrations. But what I most clearly remember, though Peter cares nothing for them, are the huge early machines of wood and iron which are set working for Sunday afternoon audiences, so that the building echoes to their deep slow rhythmical thumping. They are hostile, as machines always are, but clumsy and slow and stupid. They are like great awkward dinosaurs beside our mammalian swiftness of mind and limb, and watching them we feel the oddest mixture of contempt and fear—that these powerful monsters could crush us as easily as we can crush an egg, but that they can no more catch us than we could catch a bird by running after it.

However I have looked at the machines quite often enough already, waiting for Peter. I would much prefer the swearing. But I suppose it would not do, not with John and Peter there anyway, though it seems a pity. But parents alas, must preserve the family decencies, and I must not seem to condone the more scabrous language. Certainly I must not let the children realize how hard I have always found it to be shocked by swearing. It seems rather an endearing naïveté that young men should feel themselves such dashing fellows simply because they pick up some word which seems to them dreadful, and fling it out at us in bravado for the pleasure of our shocked disapproval. Their defiance is a tribute I suppose, and I am shocked when I can remember, but it is not always easy to remember the things young men find shocking, and what I really prefer are the vanishing race of old-fashioned white-haired gentlemen who hush up the most innocent stories "because there are ladies present."

They wear a home-grown rose in their coats, and when we cross the road together they offer me their arms with a little flourish instead of intimately taking mine. "There are ladies present," they say, and I suddenly feel myself most charmingly feminine, dressed in some becoming Edwardian style of silks and flounces, deliciously perfumed and wonderfully leisured. But alas, it becomes a rarer and rarer pleasure. It is mostly taken for granted that for wives and mothers there is nothing much left to be shocked about. Which is true of course, but dull, like one's everyday working clothes. It is pleasant to be dressed-up now and again as a leisured lady.

So I suppose the boys must go alone to the swearing-machine, and I must content myself with their censored reports at tea-time. Most reports now are censored, I cannot help feeling, and even their school essay-books are no longer the revealing evening reading they used to be. There is seldom anything now but sensible accounts of history and tedious lives of the great. Only on the first week back after the summer holidays the first essay of the autumn term is always the same: "What I did in the summer holidays." I always wonder whether the English master is insatiably curious about other people's lives, or whether it is simply that they have had no history lessons yet to set homework on, so he must find something else.

This last summer holiday both Peter and John went to live with French families, and I suddenly realize that I have never read Peter's account of his visit. John's I remember was his usual account of energetic pleasures, but what Peter made of France I am much more curious to find out. And looking through the book he has left on his desk I find it, headed as I expected: "What I did in the holidays." But his essay is a disappointment, a perfectly sensible description of the journey, and France, and family life in a French household. It is all very dull. This non-committal account is followed however by a carefully detailed assessment of the food and cooking. He should enjoy the French food and wine, so we told him before he went, and Peter takes all advice quite seriously, besides being something of a gourmet himself without any encouragement from us. But I wonder if the English master was as surprised as I was by the end of his essay—a single considered sentence set out all by itself as a separate paragraph:

"The food was good but not excellent."

No doubt that was added for everyone's amusement, but what Peter never intends is his wrong spelling, the fantastic mistakes which grow more unlikely the more he tries. For he does try most earnestly and seriously to subject his spelling to the accepted rules, and though he no longer labels his spelling-book SPPELING as he once did, yet his attempts at the most everyday of words still produce quite astonishing results.

I too am a moderately bad speller, though no real rival to Peter in original invention. And in any case I am old enough now for people not to mention my lapses, for fear of hurting my feelings. But Peter is still at an age when it is taken for granted (I wonder why?) that he has no feelings yet to be hurt. He never brings home a school report without some irritated comment from a master goaded out of patience by a term of mis-spelt work.

"His spelling is atrocious," they declare in annoyance.

"He *must* learn to spell."

"As usual his spelling is deplorable."

Then rising to a final crescendo of indignation—"His spelling is positively pre-Johnsonian."

Poor Peter. And he does try. But they are quite right, his feelings are not hurt in the least. Even the next barbed comment does not trouble him, and he reads it out aloud with a chuckle.

"A rather idle self-satisfied atmosphere has surrounded him this term." (I can see that we each have our own way of describing Peter's sea-change from anxious child to self-assured young man. The only difference is that I am relieved at the change and they are not.) Peter goes on reading:

"He really must cease playing the leisured gentleman and do more work."

But the best joke of all, though one which Peter would never see for himself, is that this censorious master, this ruthless critic of Peter's spelling, has not written "leisured" on his report, but "leasured."

But perhaps after all, that too was intended.

THE PLEASANTEST TIME OF ALL THE FAMILY day is the boys' evening bath, and of all the rooms in a house I have always thought the bathroom best for informal entertaining. Snug and intimate, warm as a greenhouse, no-one could possibly be awkward or stand-offish in a bathroom. There is nowhere more friendly, and most people I am sure, do not use their bathrooms nearly enough for social calls. For the luxurious idleness of the steamy atmosphere is the perfect setting for friendly gossip, we can talk at our ease in a bath, lazy and warm and wonderfully comfortable. I have often thought that two baths instead of one would be the perfect arrangement, for certainly sharing a single bath will not do. No matter how enormous the bath may appear before we get into it, there is never really room enough for two, we can never agree on how hot we like the water, we get in each other's way. But two baths side by side, and talk between two pink heads with eyes just level over the rims—what could possibly be pleasanter? For our best ideas always come in the bath, or perhaps it is only that in the genial air of the bathroom all our ideas seem excellent. But no matter which, with our bathroom companions we are on excellent terms always, through the mist of warm steam the world looks wonderfully friendly and comfortable.

Now We Live in London

I have always had a very particular idea of what luxury means in terms of a bathroom. No tiles or chromium-plate or machine-like efficiency, but a large room with wall-paper and pictures on the walls, a carpeted floor, and an enamel bath set before a fire. The bath is filled—and this is the ultimate extravagance—by maids bringing hot water in large enamel jugs.

It is not that I have ever known such a bathroom. I daresay they are the bathrooms of dukes at least, and only exist now in the stately homes of the very grand. But I suppose at sometime I must have read about just such a room, and remembered it ever after. So that whenever people talk about living in luxury that is what I think of—an enamel bath on a rug in front of the fire.

I realize that nowadays it would be luxury beyond the reach even of millionaires to fill and empty a bath every day by a chain of maids with jugs like fire-buckets, but still I hope that one day I shall at least have a bathroom with an easy-chair to welcome callers who drop in for a friendly talk. (For it always is friendly in bathrooms. No-one, I have always noticed, ever comes in to quarrel with us when we lie in our bath.) I know exactly the chair I want, the symbol of all vanished friendly inefficient bathrooms. It has a high back and wings, the seat is very deep because the springs have gone, and the cover is a faded flowery chintz which goes to the wash with the bath-towels and comes back every time with the pattern more faint and faded than before.

Alas, there is no room for such a chair in the bathroom here, but at least there are no tiles either, and the minimum of detested chrome. Our evening bathroom (it is a different place in the hurried morning) has the proper easy conversational air, it is the best place in the house for idle talk. It is a setting with its own peculiar life—easy-going, affectionate, with all the time in the world. The only note of urgency or asperity is when someone comes in or out and leaves the door open. For we all wander in and out idly, enjoying the general air of the day's work over and an hour's comfortable gossip before bed. Tea-time never has quite the same comfortable intimacy, sandwiched between the journey home from school and the evening's Prep. Tea-time is pleasant enough, but it is a social occasion, the talk is for the table, an exercise in social conversation; very informal certainly, but still conversation of a sort: we must consider our audience. Whereas the talk of bathroom evenings is idle gossip and we join in or not just as we please. If we feel dull we can sit and say nothing, there are no obligations.

John to-night is lying in the bath, gazing dreamily through the steam at the ceiling while Peter and I sit and do nothing.

"I can't stand Smith, can you?" But Peter is too lazy to be bothered.

"Don't know him."

There is a comfortable pause while no-one says anything, and we all go on with our separate thoughts like reading three separate books.

John stirs himself and splashes faintly.

"Yes you *do* know him. He's that one who's always singing and doesn't know any tunes."

PETER: Oh *him*. Lord no. He's frightful.

JOHN: I can't stand his red hair or the way he walks or that awful colour of his eyes.

PETER: Oh well, he can't help that.

JOHN: And I can't bear his silly voice and the way he always leaves his mouth open. (Oh dear, what else?)

PETER: Well, that's not *his* fault, it's the way he's made. You can't blame him for *that*. What *I* can't stand is that he's so affected and conceited and always showing off.

I suppose the poor boy cannot help the showing-off either, but they can scarcely realize that yet, and Peter is as tolerant as can be expected.

"But I think Brown is a decent chap for all they say."

"My dear boy, he's a rotter. Don't have anything to do with him."

"Rotter." What a delightfully old-fashioned word. Do they still say "bounder" I wonder, or "cad"? I wonder if they would enjoy P. G. Wodehouse?

"You wait till you have Mr. X to teach you." This is some school gossip of Peter's which I have missed. "He believes *anything*. Last term we told him there was a new boy called Carruthers, only he wasn't coming till the second week because he'd got measles. Then the second week we said yes, he was back, but he'd gone to Matron because he felt sick. And every day when Mr. X. called his name at roll-call we made an excuse, and every night we took it in turns to do his Prep and the same boy always copied it out because of the writing. And at the end of the term . . ."

"I don't believe it," John interrupts. As younger brother he is prepared to listen to Peter's opinion on most subjects, but this is too much. Peter leans back and grins.

"Well no. I don't suppose you do *believe* it. You're not really meant to. It's just to show you the sort of thing."

Since his transformation Peter finds his world not only manageable but constantly amusing. The self-satisfaction his formmaster complains of is not so much satisfaction with himself, but with a life where he feels himself for the first time confidently at home. About his own limitations he is still humble, the difference is that now he accepts them without anxiety.

John lies back comfortably in the bath, very pink from his energetic washing.

"At school next term" (he is asking Peter's advice from his year of experience) "shall I join the Army Corps or the Boy Scouts?"

Peter considers thoughtfully. He chose Corps himself but it has all kinds of drawbacks.

"It's an absolute *sweat* pressing trousers and doing blanco and cleaning brasses. And all that awful marching about in boots and things."

He considers in silence the prospect of avoiding such trials by being a Boy Scout instead of a soldier, but comes to a sudden impatient decision.

"It's no good, you *can't*. You just *can't* stand at attention and salute like this with half your fingers." He does a ludicrous and unkind caricature of a salute, making himself deliberately ridiculous. But I can see that it would not suit them: they are too large perhaps, or too satirical.

"All the same," Peter goes on wistfully, "it's a lovely shag life being a Scout—just sitting about all afternoon and tying knots."

No doubt Peter's idea of scouting is as uninformed as John's old idea of the Army. "What position is he?" he used to ask of officers, as if they were players in a football team. And so they were for John. In a hierarchy he once wrote out for his own convenience, Lieutenant-Colonel was changed to Left-Currnal. There was also a Right-Currnal and a Centre-Currnal. Fighting, he realized, was one of the competitive sports, and football was the only one he knew besides cricket, and cricket was clearly too tame, having no private fights.

"What our Sergeant can't understand," Peter is telling John, "is why we're so good at map-reading and calculations, when we're the worst lot he's *ever* had at drill. *Much* the worst, he says. He can't *think* what's the matter with us. But he's too particular." Peter's chuckle is so infectious that I giggle too before I even know what he will say. "We can all do the drill *perfectly* well if he'd leave us alone. It's only that we all have our own different ways of doing it. But if he'd just tell us to start off, then be patient and wait for a minute and think about something else, then he'd find we all got through it in the end."

This seems perfectly reasonable to John, who knows even less about soldiering than I do, and he lies in the bath without comment.

"With simple things like saluting," Peter goes on for me this time, since John does not appreciate the joke, "we all watch our next-door neighbour and do it when he does. It gives our saluting a very graceful wave effect all along the line. But I don't think our Sergeant appreciates *that* either."

I realize that we are back again to the Rules of Cricket of their first year in London, but now there is no division into laughed-at and laughing, they amuse themselves and each other almost equally.

"And the Army's always a century behind the times," Peter goes on. "Do you know that the Horse Guards always carry an axe instead of a sword? And why do you think they do?" He knows that neither John nor I have any idea, and he answers his own rhetorical questions. "It's for when they come to a forest, so that they can cut a way through for their sovereign."

"I see," says John, "In places like Saint John's Wood I suppose."

In the benign atmosphere of the bathroom this seems quite wonderfully witty to these newly-fledged young Londoners. It seems very funny to me too, and I shall look particularly for the axes next time I pass the Guards riding along St. James's Park in magnificent disdain, poised on their horses as aloof and exquisite as what I call mannequins (for I shall never get used to calling them models, as I shall never get used to singing God Save the Queen. And E.R. on pillar-boxes will always mean for me Edwardus Rex.)

The ones who carry the axes wear black tunics, so Peter tells us, and the axe is of carefully polished silver with a smart black handle and something engraved on the blade. They carry it upright against their shoulder like a sword, he says, and it sounds so ridiculous that I wonder whether he has made it all up perhaps, for our amusement.

John however is not interested in the Guards; he must decide about Corps versus Scouts.

"What about Field Days? Are they any good? Is it worth joining Corps for the Field Days?"

Peter encourages him with an account of their last day out, an extraordinary expedition in Peter's version, with the food far more important than the fighting. A bottle of wine one boy brought (though he forgot the corkscrew and they spent the whole journey prising out the cork with penknives), cold chicken and grapes and coffee cream-cake in a tin.

"Did you have lunch as soon as you de-bussed on the common?" John asks, with plans perhaps for lunches even more delicious, but much too bulky and elaborate to carry into battle.

"My dear good brother. We didn't de-*bus,* we de-*landing-crafted.* And it wasn't a *common,* it was a *beach.* You forget we were assault troops landing on an enemy island."

But Peter suddenly loses interest in past Field Days. It is his turn for the bath and he stirs up John from his torpor by pouring cold water from a tooth-mug on to his knees and chest—vulnerable islands unprotected by the bath-water.

"Do get out. You've been soaking for *hours,* and *I've* got to wash my hair."

There is a great heaving and splashing, and John stands up bright pink and streaming water in little runnels down his legs, grown large and muscular now, and very serviceable-looking.

"Dear Dardy." It is Peter at his most cajoling. "*Dear* Dardy." He gets the bottle of shampoo from the cupboard and puts it in my hand, wrapping my fingers round it with a little pat to keep them there. "Dardy, *please* wash my hair for me. Just this once. I know I'm *far* too old to have it done for me and I'll *never* ask you again. I'll *always* do it for myself ever after. But just this once. *Dear* Dardy."

It is an absurd weekly pantomime of "never again," and I wonder just how much longer I shall go on being their nursemaid. Already Peter begins to realize that it is a luxury to have someone to supervise his affairs, that the world is an indifferent place, where we all have to keep ourselves clean without supervision.

John is carefully weighing himself on the bathroom scales, as they both do every night with their thoughts on rowing. They weigh before they put on their pyjamas (since pyjamas would be extra weight and therefore cheating) and they both hope to gain a stone before Christmas. For they are neither of them, so they have decided, really heavy enough to pull the boat in serious rowing.

"This just won't do," John says, looking at his weight with disgust. "I haven't put on a single ounce since yesterday. I must stuff in more helpings of pudding. It was six to-day but I see I must do better."

"O, I wouldn't bother so much about how much you weigh." Peter is in the bath now, running more hot water, idly floating, benevolent. "What you should do is stand with your legs bent so you're bow-legged, and scratch yourself under your armpits and look like a gorilla. Then they'll think how tough you must be and put you straight away in the First Eight."

John tries it, bending his knees out sideways, his face twisted in a furious grimace, scratching away under his arms. He looks so absurd, bright pink still from the bath, that we laugh helplessly, and I wonder whether Peter will collapse in the water and drown.

John turns to admire his new gorilla face in the mirror, but the steamy surface reflects only a soft pink smudge with melting blue pools for eyes, delicious as a face by Renoir. And faintly, like a shadow in the mist, is the picture he drew last night in the steam on the mirror, of a pig dancing in a large top-hat, and underneath a message for his brother: PETER IS A SILLY ASS.

It will reappear I suppose, like secret writing every time we have a bath, until I clean the mirror again. And I wonder that someone has not used it in a film about a child killed suddenly, and I think how dreadful it would be if they did.

John has gone walking off bow-legged to fetch his forgotten pyjamas, and I must wash Peter's hair. But for the last time, I tell him, *certainly* for the last time. For what would the boys at school think of him I ask, trying to shame him into independence, what *would* they say if they knew his mother still washed his hair?

But Peter cares not a rap what anyone says. "I expect they'd be jealous," he says promptly. "We're all as lazy as each other if we get the chance."

And certainly we both of us know that as long as I come and join them in the bathroom I shall always fuss about washing their hair and their ears.

"Yes, of *course* the last time," Peter says grinning, lying back in the water so that his washed hair floats round his head like seaweed round a rock. John has come shivering back again into our Turkish bath, with his pyjamas under one arm and a translation of the *Iliad* under the other.

"I've found some gorgeous new bits," he tells Peter as he thrusts his legs energetically into the striped trousers of his pyjamas. "I saved them specially for the bath," he says, turning over the pages to find and read them aloud, leaning against the wall (since I am sitting on the only chair), leaning easily, languid from the heat, looking already the handsome young man he will clearly be later on.

"Meges the mighty spearman caught up this man and struck him with his sharp lance on the nape of the neck. The point came through between his jaws and severed his tongue at the root. He fell down in the dust and bit the cold bronze with his teeth."

At thirteen and fourteen John and Peter have reached the period of adolescence which comes just before the interest in true sex, the stage when they delight in violence. Tales of horror, torture, sudden death, they swallow down with the same relish as a box of chocolate creams, savouring them with a ghoulish appreciation quite detached from their kindly personalities. I too can still remember, when I was at the same stage of what I suppose I should call my sex-life, a similar delighted preoccupation with tortures. It was not that I could ever bear to see anyone hurt in practice, but the idea of violence in the abstract was a quite wonderfully exciting game. I found in some museum a little puppet show of ancient tortures, tiny cardboard figures in old-fashioned clothes like disinterested dolls, all busily engaged in a fine variety of the most unlikely torments on their cardboard victims. If you put a penny in the slot—or turned a handle, I forget which—then the puppets came to life, torturing each other with unconvincing cardboard jerks, up and down and backwards and forwards. I no longer alas, remember any of the details, only vividly a delicious half-shameful delight, which still seems the most excellent possible value for a penny.

And now the boys have reached the same stage, but are not ashamed of it in the least. John glances expertly through the pages of the *Iliad* for the passage he wants, and goes on reading with gruesome relish in his warm clear voice.

"The plumed helmet, hit by the heavy spear and the great hand behind it, was rent open by the point and the man's blood and brains came gushing through the vizor from his wound."

"Gorgeous," says Peter again, stretched out luxuriously in the hot water, half-lying, half-floating, bonelessly relaxed, his mild sensitive face smiling serenely. Gorgeous is their word of the moment and they find it covers everything they need, as "artificial" once did years ago, and a host of other words have done since. "*Gorgeous*," they say, with a long savouring emphasis on the first throaty syllable. "It's absolutely *gorgeous*." And they use it, amused, with an ever-widening range of meaning, not only as I would for a young man with too-bright ties and socks, but for a half-day holiday from school, or a tea of lavish sticky cream-buns, or the blood-and-bowels fighting in the *Iliad*.

I gave them Homer to read in one of the matey modern-style translations, for all roads lead to Rome in the education of children, and I provide them with literature instead of penny puppet-shows. For a delight in violence is not at all confined to adolescents, and they might as well share their enthusiasm with their betters. The *Iliad* is John's favourite book of the moment. He reads it out aloud, reads it passionately as befits great literature, savours and experiences it with pleasure as one should.

My own favourite reading at this same age was Poe's *Tales of Mystery and Imagination*, but this they find unexpectedly dull, and I am amused to see that there are fashions in horror just as there are in the setting of butterflies. But they enjoyed the Icelandic sagas which I cautiously offered them ("Cowards are the ones who come back from fights with all their arms and legs still on") and Defoe's *History of the Plague Year*—both hard work for pleasure I should have thought, but perhaps I did not read them at the right moment.

One of the earliest pictures I remember with enthusiasm was a large portrait of two well-fed polar bears looking complacently at the wreck of a ship on the ice; and underneath, in lettering like a Sunday-school text, it said "Man Proposes, God Disposes."

It was a most wonderful picture I thought, completely satisfying. So that clearly my early passions were ill-directed, and if it was horror pictures I wanted I could just as well have learned by heart every inch of Pallaiuolo's "Saint Sebastian" in the National Gallery, the archers violent enough for the blood-thirstiest child, Saint Sebastian elegantly languid as he always is, far more concerned with his graceful pose than he is with the arrows which pierce him like knitting-needles in all directions.

Still I dare say Saint Sebastian is not really the suitable thing for boys, and soon now they will reach the stage of sex proper; and then of course I can supply them with endless reading. And not only reading, but pictures, plays, poetry, sculpture. They will find that half the pictures in any art gallery are of young women with no clothes on, that most of the novels and poems are of love. Sex is a preoccupation they will find they share with all the world, and it will do very well as a bait to catch their enthusiasm. For so long as they become conscious of the arts it scarcely matters how. Works of art, once swallowed, live their own lives in our developing minds and sensibilities, and how they first got there does not much matter.

But the *Iliad* is finished. John has gone to bed and Peter's bath-water is growing cold.

"Dardy, *do* bully me and make me get out. I shall never have the strength to get out by myself unless you do. I'll be frozen in by morning, and then just *think* how sorry you'll be. *Please* come and bully me."

My bullying days are nearly over, thank goodness. Quite soon now I shall not bother. But Peter utters an awful warning.

"If you go away and leave me in the bath, you'll find I'm a corpse in the morning."

I pull him up by the hair, half-dry by now and hanging in rat-tails over his eyes, and from his bed in the room next-door we can hear John's voice rich and warm with satisfaction.

"Gorgeous. A man's best friend is his bed." And indeed John has a great talent for making himself comfortable, piling up his pillows, arranging the wireless and bed-light and books all within reach. "When I think," he goes on reflectively in a surprised voice, "When I think that I used to *hate* going to bed and always wanted to get up as soon as I could! I can't *believe* it. I must have been *mad*." He settles back luxuriously against his pillows and goes on with his monologue. "Of course I don't want to go to *sleep*. That's quite different. I like to come to bed and read. We often read for *hours*, you know, after you think our lights are out."

As one of the bathroom society I do not count as a parent it seems. I can be treated as a companion and relied on not to take advantage of information told me in confidence. And of course I have always known about the reading. They forget that their bedrooms have fanlights over the doors and their bed-side lamps shine down the well of the staircase, so that I know when they are reading late without coming upstairs at all. But it would be unkind to tell them so.

"We always know who's coming upstairs as soon as you start," John goes on. "When it's William it sounds like this 'Thump (pause) Thump (pause) Thump (a little grunt) Thump (pause) Thump (another grunt),'" and so on up both flights. "He takes so long that we've time to finish the chapter we're reading and go right off to sleep before he gets to the top. Most other people come up with a sort of pat, pat, pat; but when it's you there's just one long Brrr—and you're at the top. There's hardly time to turn our lights out even."

They need not worry. I am delighted to give up the supervising of lights. It is one of the more tiresome duties of mothers, and now they are leaving their childhood behind them I shall thankfully ignore whatever they do when once we have said Good night. For this last year has been one of the big leaps forward for both of them. It is as if they had moved on a generation, changing from boys to young adults. If they had to choose now which side they belonged of the dividing line between grown-ups and children, it is us they would join now I think, and not the children. The gap between twelve and fourteen is as wide as the gap between fourteen and forty, or so they seem to feel.

Nor has puberty meant sex particularly, for although our friends have lots of pretty daughters they seem not to care much yet for girls, or perhaps it is only the artificial conditions of our society which treats them as sexually children still, even though they are deep-voiced now and will soon need to shave every morning.

The character of the household too has changed in the last year: there is no longer the clear division between parents and children, but a family living together on more or less equal terms. A family with too many men I begin to feel, sighing for the sisters and daughters I have never had. And this week there are more men than ever, for an architect brother has come to London to take exams. The house in fact seems full of people taking exams, for Peter and John too are at the end of their school year, with papers to answer each morning and afternoon. They all three come in for tea together, important and cheerful and very hungry, and although they will eat a large supper later on, it makes no difference at all to the amount of tea they all eat now. In an astonishingly short time the tea-table is a ravaged desert of crumbs and empty plates, and they loll back in their chairs, stretching out their six long legs under the table, supremely at their ease, as only the young and supple can be at ease on hard kitchen chairs.

It is a useless torment of spirit, they long ago decided, to discuss one's own examination questions when once it is all over. But other people's are a different matter entirely, and they exchange papers with princely nonchalance, Physics and Latin and Maths and History and questions on fascinating unlikely architectural subjects like Gardening and Geology.

Their own paper of course was exceptionally difficult, but any of the others they could have answered perfectly well, they are reassured to find. For we always *can* solve other people's problems: the questions we need not answer are always most provokingly easier than the ones we need. It is one of the particular minor pleasures to read other people's examination papers, to skim quickly over the questions we know nothing of, and pronounce with patronizing self-confidence that Really, this was a *gift* of a paper, even *we* could have done quite well if *this* is all that's expected.

It is the most shameless boasting of course, but then they know quite well that their knowledge is never going to be put to the test by setting it down in words and handing it in to be marked. And it does them all good to boast a little after the private ordeals of their day, especially such harmless boasting as this, for no-one listens to anything the others say. This is not conversation at all, but three separate people making three separate noises for their own satisfaction.

But they soon grow tired of boasting, and we ask each other what we shall do for the rest of the evening. It is folly, we are all agreed, to do any work while examinations are going on. The important thing, so we tell each other, all of us smiling in perfect agreement, the one thing that matters above all else in examinations is to come to them completely *fresh*. It is a theory I have always most enthusiastically believed in, setting such store by the freshness that lest it should be in any way staled I would shut up all books with a sigh of relief a week or more before any examination I ever took. It was a week I always looked forward to, a week of the idlest and most delightful pleasure, enhanced by the constant satisfaction of playing truant while everyone else was feverishly working.

There is no need however to put such ideas into John's head. He has ideas enough of his own, enough to turn the whole year to holiday if only he had his way. But what shall we do to-night? It is summer and daylight and invitingly warm, and since William will not be in for an evening meal, and since my brother is seldom in London, we will take him out we decide, and drive him round the town. But where shall we go? for we all have our favourite places. Shall we go up the hill to Hampstead? climbing steeply up the narrow street to Whitestone Pond on the top, so high and airy and like a cliff above the far blue sea of the city below that I listen always for the expected cries of seagulls. It is what Peter likes best, not for the view, since adolescents are seldom admirers of views, but for the fringe of small boys and fathers always round the pond sailing elaborate model boats across the miniature ocean.

Or shall we go to Richmond Park? still so astonishingly Tudor. Or climb into a derelict cemetery which always fascinates John? the crumbling mausoleums drowned every summer in a feathery tide of enormous horsetails, which rise like a green mist about the graves. He likes to peer through the cracks of the tombs hoping for skulls, and lose himself in narrow green paths through the forest of horsetails brushing his chin.

But no. Tombs are no way to entertain a visitor. We will go to the river as we always do, making always for the water in the end, no matter which way we set out. For the London Thames, like Cleopatra, has infinite variety which custom does not stale. Will the tide be up or down? we wonder. But the boys can tell us: they have a list of high tides always in their pockets for rowing—it is one of the charms of their rowing, that it links us with the sea. The tide will be full they say, and so it is when we get there, the river brimming mysteriously with its purposeful up and down currents, so that a dead cat, Peter tells us with relish, is carried up and down ten times under London Bridge before it disappears.

Surely, I think, I have heard that before. Though it was seven times up and down I think. Or was it only three? But someone else has told me, standing on a bridge one evening like this. Perhaps it was William, and perhaps he told Peter. But this is not London Bridge in any case, so perhaps we shall escape the cats —or was it dogs perhaps? It is Westminster Bridge where we are leaning over the parapet, four of us in a row looking at the views —pure Whistler upstream, pure Canaletto down. But the downstream view is so astonishingly historical, so full of famous pictures, that it scarcely seems reasonable for the dome of Saint Paul's to float over the scene in ordinary daylight as it does in so many paintings in so many picture galleries. But then it never is ordinary daylight over the river, with the mists and the reflected light and the shimmering water and the great open span of the sky. The London Thames is always half mirage. And I think how much more romantic and mysterious it is, for all its squalor, than the Seine at Paris. For the Seine is a garden river, tidy and decorous, with no tides or mud-flats or strange dark life: a drawing-room river, elegant and beautiful certainly, but dull and unromantic after the Thames; like a carefully laid-out park beside the true mysterious country.

The boys are making bets with my brother, balancing the pennies in a row along the parapet of the bridge, bets on whether the neat black police boat, hurrying upstream towards us like a water-beetle, will pass under the arch of the bridge where we are standing or under the next one. They do complicated calculations on how much beforehand they would have to jump to land exactly on the middle of its cabin roof as it passed beneath. And they seem to me astonishingly clever, for I was never good at sums I think, gazing idly at the dome of Saint Paul's. Now they are all congratulating each other on the excellent Maths exams they would all be able to set, but I only half-listen, trying for the hundredth time to get used to the idea that when one looks at them from any distance, both Saint Paul's and the Houses of Parliament are always on the wrong side of the river.

But my companions are tired of their river games. They do not care about Canaletto, and they are all of them too young to appreciate the Victorian Gothic of the Houses of Parliament—even my architect brother, if he dared to confess it, is too young yet to care very much about anything older than himself. Which is no doubt just as it should be.

We pack ourselves into the car again, the boys folding up their long legs like grasshoppers into the back seat, for my own legs are as long as theirs, and I keep my driving-seat pushed most unfairly far back. We will go to the Festival Hall we decide, for my brother has never seen it, and I never tire of the brave new world atmosphere of its entrances and staircases and galleries looking out into the night of the river. Perhaps it is that listening to music makes our mind more receptive to other arts, but certainly no other building I have been in has given me so vividly the sense of a new aesthetic. Here at last, halfway through the century, is our new way of seeing and feeling and living.

But can't I remember, my companions want to know, all of us

standing together in the entrance of the auditorium, can't I remember anything at *all* of the lecture William once took me to on the building of the Festival Hall? *Think*, they tell me, and they give my arm a little shake to bring back my wandering attention, for it is acoustics they are interested in, not atmospheres.

"Well," I tell them, "the architects never really knew what it would sound like till they played some music in it and tried."

Yes, they say, Yes. They are very patient. But what after all can that count for as information?

There was something about echoes, I tell them, and different-sized bottles sunk in the roof to catch them—but that was in Mediæval churches perhaps, not here, and how can I expect them to believe anything which sounds so absurd? But it was the echo they thought of always, I remember, as their likeliest and deadliest enemy; haunted even in sleep perhaps by the truly magnificent echo of the Albert Hall. And indeed that echo is a most powerful ghost, with a life of its own so vital that I never pass the Albert Hall without feeling that the dome is singing endlessly to itself, ghostly echo performances of *Hiawatha* in the summer and the *Messiah* in the winter.

My family are resigned at last to my ignorance and after all, why should *I* know? Why do they expect *me* to know about acoustics? They are impatient now to be off, and we drive back fast and triumphant northwards over Waterloo Bridge and into the canyon City, empty now at night, so that for anyone who has nosed his way a yard at a time through the daytime congestion, it is wonderfully exhilarating to drive straight through the narrow streets without stopping, and out into the East End beyond.

The East End of London is not at all how we expect it to be. It is quiet and spread-out and lonely. Or so it is at night. By day it may be noisy and crowded, but it must always be more spacious than anything we are used to at the other end of the town. In the City and central London we accept it as natural that everything should push in closely together at the centre. We take it for granted that all the buildings will be piled up high, that the roads and pavements will be crowded always. Every square foot of land is precious, and a £5 note, they used to say, would buy no more than the ground it covered. But that was long ago, and now goodness knows how many notes it would need, so that even the smallest open space in front of a building seems the greatest luxury and extravagance, and a perverse part of our pleasure in the central parks is the knowledge that they must be guarded inch by green inch from the encroaching town, as fiercely as we guarded our childhood sand-castles from the rising tide. It gives a wonderfully exotic air to even the sootiest patch of grass and bushes.

But the East End is not like that. Suddenly after the bank-note City the East End is streets of little houses, and the first thing we notice always is the sky. Not strips and patches of blue, not broken oddments glimpsed between buildings as it is with us, but a great open arch of empty sky with the streets lying quietly beneath. For these are little houses built for families to live in before space was precious. The streets are wide by City standards, the houses low—only two floors mostly—and often between the houses and the street there is a tiny patch of garden and a tree. So although in this poorer part of the town there are sadly few parks, yet still there is far more green than we ever would have expected. And by London standards this part of the town is quiet. There are no big shops to draw people in from outside, no theatres or restaurants or offices with their bustling population of migrants, not much traffic off the main roads of lorries and buses, as there is round us, packed tight in every side-street. And the feeling of the old villages is still strong, of the old parishes with their churches remote now and set in green, withdrawn and solitary and beautiful.

To-night the East End is very quiet and empty in the long summer twilight, the young people lured away I suppose to Piccadilly Circus and Leicester Square, drawn as irresistibly as any villagers by the lights and life of the other end of the town. But we have come across to this end—so perverse are human beings —to wind through the narrow streets of high gaunt warehouses which are the best of all Victorian architecture if only people would look at them and see.

On the Isle of Dogs we come out at the river, but it used to be so damp, so an old doctor told me once, that when he worked here long ago the houses were infested with slugs as other people's houses were infested with beetles. It is one of the few places in the East End where we can get to the river and the Docks, open and clean and swept, with their breezy air of the sea. Once when they were little, I tell the children, I brought them here to see the ships. And because they had just learned to read they read out aloud the names of all the ships they could see. CAROLA it said in clean white letters on the side of the nearest, and underneath it said HULL. "I can't see why they need write Hull," said John with the scorn of a confident six-year-old. "I'm sure the sailors know which part's the hull without having to tell them."

But this is not a funny story except to my brother and me. The boys are not in the least amused, but seem rather embarrassed that I should take so childish a pleasure in puns. Perhaps even at their present great age they do not yet feel safe enough from such naïvetés to laugh at them with any confidence. Besides, growing older is like growing out of fashions, nothing is so unsympathetic to us as the age we have just left behind. It is one of the fundamental facts in the history of taste which even children realize. "You know," Peter said to me at Christmas, "it's a good thing we didn't send that clockwork steam-roller to Nicky. He's *just* got too old for it now, and nothing's as boring as toys you've *just* got too old for."

My companions are tired now of the deserted Docks. Is there time, they ask, to go through the Blackwall Tunnel and out to Greenwich? But no. It is too late. We must turn round now and at least head towards home again: however often we may still stop on the way, we must at least be travelling in the right direction. And we stop often: to watch the slow-motion of Tower Bridge opening for a ship to pass, to seek out secret squares and gardens hidden behind non-committal street-fronts, and near Saint Paul's to explore an enormous new pit they are digging out with all the splendid bull-dozers and grabs and mechanical shovels—all the magnificent toys which builders must so delight in.

It is a fascinating hole to find in the middle of the City, and who knows? if we look carefully we may discover the corner of another Roman temple. My athletic companions have found a gap where they can climb through, and swing along the railings to drop down what seems to me a terrifying height on to a pile of sand, and make their way into the excavations far below.

How they are ever to get back again I cannot imagine, but I wait for them on the bridge which spans this end of the hole, mildly alarmed to feel how it throbs gently but unmistakably every time a bus passes over. What is there underneath I wonder, if we all go through? But I am reassured to remember that during the day half a dozen buses must often pass all at once without mishap, and I feel safe enough to consider instead the enormous bulk of Saint Paul's rising like a natural growth of rock at the other side of the hole. All town architecture has this in common I think (is it because of my architect companion I wonder, that to-night especially I notice the buildings?)—at its best town architecture does not put up separate units, but creates stretches of urban landscape. It is not only in the town-planning of streets and squares, but also when single buildings are conceived as part of the architecture of a town, they are not self-contained units in an open space (as a house is for instance, set in a garden) but integrated parts of the urban scene. There in front of me is Saint Paul's, like a mountain range in the landscape of London, a magnificent and complicated out-crop of stone pushing superbly through the untidy general level of the town: cliffs of walls, pinnacle-peaks, plateau-roofs, precipices, ridges, valleys; and rising enormous above them—a mountain above its foothills, Mount Everest to London—the huge majestic dome.

Nor is it only Saint Paul's, but most of the buildings we remember as London's finest have this feeling of being natural landscape formations. Perhaps, I think (seeing no sign in the hole of my three lost passengers, not liking to shout loudly enough to summon them back, resigned to my waiting), perhaps it is the one essential of all good town architecture, since buildings are the very stuff of cities, as hills and woods and fields are the stuff of country landscapes. The Houses of Parliament, the Horse Guards from St. James's Park, Somerset House like a cliff along the river—these are not separate buildings, but stretches of noble landscape. The National Gallery is the side of a square, a varied but homogeneous façade so perfectly suited to its site that we never think of it as a detached building, but as the north side of Trafalgar Square.

It is what is the matter with the Festival Hall I decide, remembering how awkwardly it sits by the river, thinking how many hours of my life I have spent like this, waiting for boys to come back. The Festival Hall is not yet successful from the outside because it is a separate entity unrelated to the surrounding urban landscape. Perhaps when the other buildings are round it the whole group will take root and grow into the South Bank.

My three lost companions have climbed back at last, returned like Persephone from the underworld, ready for home, hungry, bringing me flints, not chipped they are sure by any river current, but by some remote ancestor squatting on this lonely river bank, watching the marshes of the valley for enemies or food.

All three of them have a raffish dishevelled air, and their black town shoes are so thick with wet mud that I wonder in housewifely fashion whether they will dry in time to clean for school to-morrow. For neither of the boys can have spare pairs of school shoes until their feet stop growing a size or more every term. I am tired of the bottoms of their wardrobes full of only half-worn shoes.

Yes, they grant me, for we are discussing which way we shall go home—Yes, we will go back through Covent Garden and look at the flowers. They are not really interested: they want their supper. But I have after all, been "jolly decent," waiting about while they climbed into holes, driving them round wherever they fancied. And the flowers are my reward, the market flooded with lakes of blossom, piled masses of bloom, streets and roads whose boundaries are not buildings but ranged banks and terraces of thousands and thousands of flowers, all grown to their lavish best to come to London.

There are flowers in pots as if for a show, flowers in bunches all facing the same way as if for a camera, flowers arranged on stalls in tiers one above the other to face an audience. It is an assembly, a celebration, a grand court function of flowers for a midsummer festival. And in the cloistered warmth and stillness of the evening beneath the roof, the fragrance gathers like an invisible mist, lies in pools between the banks of blossom, drifts down the aisles in waves of heavy sweetness. And drowned with colour, drunk with fragrance, I have the vividest conviction that these flowery presences are sending out strange vibrations which our mere mortal senses cannot perceive. Their colours perhaps, vibrate in the air as notes of music if only we had the right ears to catch them; the crimsons full and sonorous, the whites serene, the blues insistent—blues changed to vivid violet under the neon lamps, irises and pansies and cornflowers and hydrangeas glowing with so intense a light that I gaze at their penetrating colour, half expecting to hear some clear high note of unearthly sound.

But haven't I seen enough? my companions interrupt me impatiently, standing dark and indifferent against the blossoming background. Aren't I ready to go home? they ask, and the roses bloom about their shoulders. They are hungry they say, heading me off from entrancing flowery vistas, steering me towards the doors, one on each side of me and one behind like benign but determined policemen.

They know very well that I am mounted on my gardening hobby-horse, and that unless they keep firm hold of me I shall gallop off by myself and leave them to go home alone. They are hungry, they tell me again.

But what do I care when there are lilies all about us? And No, they answer patiently, as if I were a child to be humoured, No. They think they'd better not go and buy hot dogs and coffee at the market-stall as I suggest, because if they leave me alone they complain, then I am sure to buy a blue hydrangea. And if I buy *one* hydrangea they explain, then I must buy a dozen, and how can they, they ask pathetically, how *can* they get twelve large hydrangeas in the car when they can scarcely get in themselves?

But we could nurse them on our knees, I think to myself, hold them between our feet, pile them on the roof. Suddenly I see us driving back in triumph through the town, a moving barrow of hydrangeas shining blue in the lights all the way across Bloomsbury and home.

They have got me almost to the door by now, and I sigh resignedly, for I am disciplined by all the years of domesticity to a mild and reasonable creature. But all the same, if the market porters were not so clearly anxious to be rid of us I would not go so meekly, just because my three young men are hungry again and want to take me back as a cook to make them omelettes for supper. I would tell them to walk home, or catch a bus: to go home and find their own supper for once; and I would follow when I was ready, with hydrangeas for passengers instead of large creatures with muddy boots.

Not really that I am very fond of hydrangeas, coarse and shapeless flowers which almost might be sold by weight, so heavy are their bloated heads of blossom. But nothing else so perfectly evokes the London summer season as banks of hydrangeas artificially blue. And in the market lights even their synthetic colour is strange and magical, and the family are wise indeed not to leave me alone.

Here we are. Out. And the porters have shut the doors thankfully behind us. Feeling safe at last my guards let go of my elbows and leave me to walk as I like. But the fragrance has followed us into the open, mingled now with the tropical smell of bananas and oranges from the fruit market next door, and I wish we lived near enough for the waves of scented air to come drifting in at our bedroom windows on summer nights.

But once in the car I care nothing for hydrangeas or the smell of any oranges. I want to go home. I am tired of wandering aimlessly about the town. I am like a horse headed back to its stable: we will all go home as fast as the traffic lights will let us.

Yet even when the omelettes are cooked and eaten, when the coffee is finished and there is no fruit left in the bowl nor biscuits in the tin, when even the bread and cheese is what my grandmother used to call far-sought-into, even then my three companions still sit about the untidy table reluctant to break up the evening. They talk and talk, avoiding all dangerous silences, for Peter and John know from of old that if they leave me to gather my wits I shall sooner or later look at my watch and say with horror, "Do you know what time it is?" And they both know perfectly well what time it is: it is long past bedtime. But I am too tired to care. They can stay up all night if they like, as long as they stay up without me. For I shall go to bed and dream of my lost hydrangeas.

"HELL AND DAMNATION AND THE DEVIL TAKE the hindmost." It is a cheerful voice from the kitchen, and reaches me out in the yard where I am planting the garden tubs with daffodils for next spring. For even after all these years in London I still keep my exaggerated country consciousness of the coming seasons.

"Hell." It is a deep male voice—what William would call a hairy voice—but it might belong to any of them now, for the boys have grown as tall and hairy-voiced as their father, and with their new men's voices have taken on new men's expressions as if by the same biological development.

"Damn-Damn-Damn." This time it is John protesting, but they are all three in the kitchen making tea (I can hear the rattle of cups and saucers) and to judge by the fuss they are making they must be pouring the hot water into their shoes instead of the teapot. Clearly no one is hurt, or they would not waste time on such elaborate protesting; but how awkward men are, I tell myself, and can never make themselves comfortable. And I think how pleasant it would be to have a nice domestic daughter to do some of the mothering instead of me.

The CHEERFUL DAY

I go on with my daffodil-planting, keeping carefully to the far end of the yard where I hope they cannot see me from the kitchen window. For to-day I am in private revolt from family affairs. To-day is the boys' first day back at school after two months' holiday, a red-letter day in every housewife's year, owed us we feel, as well-earned leisure to use for our own private amusement. After breakfast the family all go off and the day is our own for the first time for months.

It is not that we do not love them all dearly; indeed the boys' company is a pleasure more satisfactory every year. But we can, so we discover with half-guilty surprise, be quite happily parted from the loved ones for the time being, can pass the day contentedly from breakfast till tea-time with no sense of loss. By the end of the holidays their company is a pleasure which for the moment we have savoured to the full: we are ready for a change. Besides, the last days of the summer holidays are a strain on the very best of relations. There are so many last-minute things to get ready, lost books to find, forgotten suits to fetch from the cleaners, new geometry sets to buy (for geometry sets have a short mysterious life never longer than a term). John has lost his white rowing sweater and cannot *think* where he had it last. Peter has grown out of his new school shoes. I have put their health certificates in a safe place and cannot find them as usual. There are dozens of missing buttons to sew on, horrible holes in the bottoms of pockets, name-tapes on awkward garments like gym shoes and belts, and a host of things which should have been done at the end of term, but were flung away in corners and forgotten in the first fine careless rapture of the holidays.

It is odd too, and depressing, how the relationship between us all relapses to the irritable friction we all of us grew out of long ago. The boys argue and bicker with each other, and I am the old impatient mother annoyed by my tiresome children. We are all in a crotchety state of boredom and irritation. Yet in a curious way we are all doing it on purpose. We could all be reasonable if we wanted, and we none of us take the least offence at this superficial bickering. It is just that we have always got ready for school like this and it seems the natural way. I scold, they grumble, and the things get done.

By contrast it gives the first day of term a wonderful sense of household peace and leisure. Off they go—quite unnaturally early in the morning, since they both have a hundred things to do before school—and when they have gone the whole long day is mine until evening. Of course there is a pile of washing waiting, summer clothes to put away, and the house to clear up after the holiday occupation. But to-day is for my own personal pleasure and nothing else till the evening meal. I think every mother must feel on the first day of term a delicious guilty sense of relief; as if we were playing truant and had slipped off to enjoy ourselves in secret. The first day of the autumn term should always be a private celebration, we should always arrange some special pleasure for ourselves. And no matter how simple and innocent our day, it is always irradiated by a feeling of guilty enjoyment which is never quite so reliable and satisfactory on any other occasion.

To-day I have done nothing except go to a flower-show and idle round the fashionable shops. But simply to go to the shops without a shopping-list in my pocket is a luxury in itself. I have bought nothing at all but a huge bunch of grapes from a barrow, and a bagful of daffodil bulbs for the yard. Even the evening meal to-day will be eggs and bacon and anything I can find in the cupboard. To-day I refuse to be responsible for any of my family.

"You'd better not tell that to Dardy or other such saints." I am curious to know what William can think me too saintly to hear, but certainly not curious enough to go in and join their tea-making.

There is silence for a time until John's head comes cheerfully through the open window with the smell of toast.

"Hello, Dardy. I wasn't going to notice you, but are there any chocolate biscuits?" He grins at me. "William wants to know," he adds, but we are both quite well aware that it is really John who fancies chocolate biscuits instead of burnt toast, and that he is only using the unsuspecting William as a lever to get me away from my planting and into the kitchen to look after them.

I sigh and leave my daffodils regretfully, and go in to see how much mess they have made between them. But first I must hear the news of the day.

"This-afternoon I was out sculling," Peter tells me, "and the water was so rough with the high tide that the boat capsized and I fell in the river."

I exclaim as I am expected to, and shudder with true sympathetic horror at the cold. "How *awful*," I say, "you poor wretched thing."

Although Peter enjoys my sympathy, he is honest. "I didn't really mind the falling-in you know. I was so hot from sculling that I scarcely noticed the cold. And besides, I climbed out straight away and sat on the bottom of my turned-up boat and *clouds* of steam went up off my rowing vest. The part I *didn't* like though was when they came to rescue me. They couldn't get the launch near enough for me to climb off my boat on to theirs, so I had to dive in again and swim. That really was *foul*."

I can quite see that this is no time of the year for river-bathing, with mists already night and morning, and the shops full of warm clothes for winter. But Peter seems less impressed by his watery adventure than by the fact that on this first day back he has Prep to do.

"It's un*heard*-of. Prep on the first day! Disgusting. And not just ten minutes' reading either, but enough to take all evening." And to show me he is in earnest he stumps off upstairs after John, who had heard about the river already and gone off before.

There is time to finish my daffodils before supper, though out in the yard it is almost too dark now to see where to plant them. But as my eyes grow used to the dusk, I can make out the white tubs by the evening light of the sky, the soft glow reflected from all the myriad lights of London, a dusky apricot which shines on the blackness of the night like an illuminated veil drawn over the dark sky behind. I can just see to plant the last tub, and to gather the tea-towels hanging on the line to dry. And standing in the dark yard under the glowing sky, I listen for the hundredth time to the mysterious murmur of London's traffic all around me, faint but unceasing on every side, strangely exciting. The city, we feel at this evening hour, is a huge living creature and we are inside it, and this faint roar of the traffic is the roar of blood flowing in the city's veins. And suddenly I am conscious of the enormity of London, of how small and separate our family life is, and how compact; that though we are part of the city, as a grain of wheat is part of a heap of corn, yet we are self-contained too as the grain is, we have our own particular flavour. And looking up at the lighted windows of the house like a cliff above me, seeing figures vaguely moving in the rooms beyond, half-hearing the familiar family voices, I remember a phrase I once read— *"Cette petite civilisation qu'est ma vie."* And watching the movements beyond the windows, the family unconscious and preoccupied in the rooms behind, I think how that is what a household is, a tiny civilization living in this house like a plant in its pot. There is William's work as a doctor, the children growing up into men, and their lives and mine are drawn together in a household world with its own domestic laws and organization. And like every family, every civilization however small and humble, we have our own particular personality, our ways of doing the ordinary things, our own prejudices and enthusiasms and family relationships. The way we arrange our house is unmistakably ours, the kind of books we read, the friends we make, the way we spend our leisure, our attitude to things that happen, even the jokes we make at meals. These are things we do—as every family does—in a way peculiarly our own.

The CHEERFUL DAY

Once when the children were little during the war I found them an old dolls'-house and furnished it for them, made curtains and rugs from scraps of cloth and carpet, chairs and beds and tables from odds and ends of wood. The children arranged it to suit their idea of domestic life, chose rooms for the parlour and the nursery, the kitchen and the hall. And if he had found it suddenly anywhere in the world, William said laughing when he came back and saw it, he would have known at once that this was quite unmistakably our own family house.

It is not that anyone is conscious of their microcosm while they are inside it, any more than living in England we are conscious of the character of England. It is only when we go abroad—to other countries, other households—that the particular flavour of what we have left is defined and made clear by the difference of our new setting. So that we come back to our own lives with the intimate pleasure of being at home again in our own indigenous atmosphere, like fish in our own small pond.

Cette petite civilisation, I think, looking at the windows and the dimly moving figures. And all families must have this same sense of a tiny community, since the family is so fundamental a unit. But there are some individual people too who can create lives with that particular organization of the business of living, can give to everything they do the characteristic flavour of an individual personality, which makes of their existence a tiny separate culture.

When we try consciously to do anything at all with our lives apart from the lives of other people, I suppose that is what we try to do: to express what we think and feel through the medium of living. History is full of such artists in living, but any life would do as the stuff of our work of art if only we were artists. But of course we are not; and the business of living is a complex and subtle medium, as intractable and far more perishable than words or paint or marble. Nor are we even conscious most of the time, of what we are making of our lives, but only fitfully in sudden visions, when for some reason we lift our ostrich heads from the sand of day-to-day preoccupations and look out over the landscape.

Then for a moment, before we burrow back again, we see what it is we are doing with our life as a whole. They are moments to be feared always: happy sometimes, but sometimes dreadful: sudden realizations of failure and futility and despair: defenceless moods of darkness not long to be borne—the moments of suicide.

Yet sometimes they are happy, sometimes suddenly and blindingly happy: visionary flashes when we see stretched out around us the whole pattern complete and satisfying, and go back content to the blinkered workaday of ordinary living, knowing the pattern is there however dimly and seldom we may catch sight of it. For most of our days are like laying the bricks of a house, dully and tediously, with only an obstinate blind faith in the intangible values of the plan we cannot see. I think it was C. Day Lewis who wrote a poem I once found:

> . . . And though my to-days are
> Repetitive, dull, disjointed,
> I must continue to practise them over and over
> Like a five-finger exercise,
> Hoping my hands at last will suddenly flower with
> Passion and harmonize.

I copied it down on the back of a writing-pad long ago in the endless lonely war-time years of housework and baby-minding —the years of the practising over and over, without even knowing for certain that there would ever be any life left afterwards to play the tune in when I had learned it. Not that there is any particular virtue in the practising, for we are all of us hard-working creatures of routine: women endlessly shop and cook and patiently train their children, men go off day after day to the steady drudgery which underlies even the most interesting work.

And sometimes our repetitive days do flower with passion, do harmonize. Suddenly, as he says, on a day like any other, for no reason at all we are suddenly blinded by a dazzle of happiness, of pleasure in what we have created. Hearing William's voice perhaps, laughing with the children in the kitchen; or the boys themselves, untroubled, intelligent, surveying with princely confidence the delights of their lives stretching ahead; or perhaps a sudden consciousness of the house so pleasant and smoothly running, and the voices of friends on the evening doorstep.

For a moment we are beyond the screen of immediate preoccupations which shuts in our view. We see with sudden brilliant happiness what it is we have been building with our patient blind laying of brick on dull brick. Yet even these dazzling bright moments are shadowed with sadness, with the inescapable knowledge that these blossomings of our lives are so intangible, so quickly over and lost. Since we are neither poets nor painters nor anything else, our moments of happiness have no expression, they exist only as a fleeting mood, half-remembered in the consciousness of people busy with other things. They are like fish which jump from the water for a second and are lost again.

Nor is it only our moods which pass, but soon too this small household world we have all of us created and shared will be gone: our tiny domestic civilization will disappear with no trace left but a faint fading vision in the memories of people who will die too in their turn. Other families will live here after us as others have lived before, and all our lives alike will vanish and be lost, our cheerful day obliterated in the everlasting night of dumb forgetfulness. Herrick wept to see the fading daffodils, but we are the flowers themselves, conscious that we perish.

I stand too long in the evening yard, gazing at the sky with my hands full of clothes-pegs and the dry linen tea-towels stiff over my arm. I must go back into my household, for my day of private holiday is over, and the children need all kinds of things done before school to-morrow. How absurd it is though, still to call

Peter and John the children, with their bristly chins and deep voices and eyes on a level with mine. But what else? Youths will not do with its suggestion of delinquents; young men sounds too like a shop for clothes, and to call them always the boys seems to insist too much on their not being girls, which is a pity. Peter and John I suppose it must be, though I shall no doubt call them the children for years yet before I remember. It is only in the last few months, so they tell me, that I have remembered at last to talk of their Prep instead of their homework.

The growing-up of children is curious: not a steady upward curve as we might expect if we had never had children of our own, but a series of sudden jumps with level stretches in between. It is as if they climbed a hill, not by walking up an even slope, but by leaping from one ledge to the next, pausing on each level terrace to get used to the new height and gather their forces for the next upward spring. Not that there has been much pausing in the last year or two. They have rushed uphill as they rush upstairs, two at a time. They are suddenly masculine, as little boys before puberty seldom are, being often more feminine than little girls, who are certainly larger and stronger at the same age. It annoyed John and Peter for years, that although at school they are larger than average, yet beside the daughters of our friends they were small and slight; that girls of their age could run faster, jump higher, swim better—were altogether tougher than boys. But now John and Peter have passed their feminine rivals. In this journey of physical growing-up they have suddenly now, at fourteen and fifteen, surged ahead beyond fear of overtaking.

As for the different stages which are the milestones of their journey, some of them are the obvious ones: learning to walk and talk, going to school, catching the spotty diseases of childhood, learning to read, changing schools, going away alone, the first long school trousers, their voices breaking, the first razor. All these are the obvious stages on the way of growing-up, a list which anyone could make by taking thought, without ever knowing any actual children. But looking back over their nine years of growing since we came to London, I can see that there are other milestones just as important which I should never have guessed. There is a transition for instance, every bit as definite as puberty, when they change from bouncing small children who wake in the early morning, to boys who sleep in so soundly that only the most determined shaking will rouse them, animals as difficult to get out of their beds as winkles out of their shells. Nor, once awake, are they any longer restless and fidgety as small children are, no more able to stay still than a bicycle can balance without moving. There are still bursts of exuberant energy, especially in the morning, bouts of larking and rough-and-tumble when it seems that any room they are in must be destroyed as if by an explosion, and I am astonished always to find that they never so much as knock over a chair. But between the explosions they can sit now for hours without moving, enthralled in what they are doing, or reading with the entire concentration of young people, which makes them as blind and deaf to outside disturbance as if they were asleep in bed in the morning.

What they read is changing too, a milestone this which they themselves recognize quite clearly. He was too old now, John suddenly decided one morning at breakfast, *much* too old for children's comics. From now on, he said, he would read the grown-up comics instead; and off he went to the paper-shop on the way to school to cancel his weekly order for space comics and ask for *Punch* to come instead. He has always been most lordly about having his comics delivered. He orders them very seriously from the newsagent, and they await him on the table in the hall on the way to breakfast, highly-coloured nonsense laid out decorously between the *Times* and the *New Statesman*. But what he would really like, so he tells me now, the paper he really prefers above all others is *The New Yorker. Far* better than *Punch*, he says, but *far* too dear. And he sighs. "It really *is* too dear you know. At school we had a committee meeting to see if we could afford it for the common-room. But we decided we couldn't. We never have much funds anyway, and we've still got to pay for that window we broke larking about last term, and if there's anything left we wanted to buy some jam for our bread at tea. So it's just no good," he says with a sigh, "but it's an awful shame."

As for Peter, his new reading territory was revealed to him with dramatic suddenness, an exhilarating prospect of delightful new country stretching unexpectedly ahead for as far as he can see. He came home one day in the oddest mood of surprise and delight. They had read Wilde's *The Importance of Being Earnest* in the English lesson, he said, and although he still chuckled with appreciation as he remembered it, his chief reaction was astonishment.

"Are the books *you* read *often* as funny as that?" he asked. "Are there any more you think I'd like?"

I suppose we all begin with the feeling that the classics are heavy old-fashioned books specially preserved by schools to be set as penitentially dull texts for examinations. It had never occurred to Peter that anyone might *enjoy* them. Do I think he will ever like reading poetry, or listening to music, or looking at pictures? Peter asks as simply and seriously as if they were sizes of shoes which he may grow to in the next year, or perhaps the year after. But he realizes now for the first time that they are all there as extra pleasures if only he can get to like them.

Novels, I thought, were the most likely to start with, and I set him off on an extensive cross-country journey through English fiction, where he has found Jane Austen so very much to his liking that the six volumes of her novels are the first six items on his list of Christmas presents. But already he is finding that the Promised Land has its limitations. Jane Austen for one thing did not write nearly enough. And also, when we start on Russian fiction it is better not to begin with *War and Peace* but with something less god-like. For it was *War and Peace* Peter found on the shelf, and was lost for a whole sleep-walking week-end while he devoured all three volumes without stopping. But *War and Peace* alas, is not a yardstick for ordinary measuring, not a random sample and all the rest just as good, as Peter has found. He still reads any Russian translations he comes across, but with a mildly rueful air now, as if not expecting too much.

War and Peace and *The New Yorker*. I can see that we shall soon all be quarrelling about the same books, and who shall read them first when new ones come from the library. As for their work at school, the children outdistanced us long ago. Neither William nor I can help any longer with their homework—it is another of the milestones, though they have either not noticed it, or if they have they at least are too polite to comment. They know as much Latin now as ever I did, and far more than I can remember. Their Maths has reached the stage of mysterious symbols as strange to me as hieroglyphs, and as for Chemistry, I remember nothing at all except coating one side of a piece of glass with some orange powder which changed it to a mirror.

When they are puzzled it is each other the children ask now, not their poor ignorant parents, and in the evenings William and I go jaunting off on pleasure, leaving them studiously working. It seems an odd arrangement. When we come back they are often still working, but how much playing about has gone on while we were out I never know. A good deal I suspect, since they seldom complain of too much homework, and they certainly would if they had worked without stopping from supper till bedtime. But I no longer interfere with the evening arrangements of such responsible citizens. I only scold them mildly off to bed to get them out of the bathroom before we want it ourselves. But quite soon now—I can see it approaching as another milestone—William and I will go to bed first and leave the bathroom to them.

They live in the household like adults now, waiting for the

evening meal with us instead of devouring a huge and varied tea as soon as they come in from school. It is one of the important and unexpected stages—this progression from tea to supper—not simply a change of meals but a change of status. They are no longer children given schoolroom tea and got rid of, but adults who share the evening meal not only with us but with visiting friends. Our old tea-time news has changed to supper-table talk, and they even now and again remember to brush their hair without telling before they come to table.

Indeed they begin lately to take a slight interest in their clothes for the first time. Already Peter cherishes a pale blue tie, and when we go to buy John a new sweater he has to be steered away from a taste in gaudy stripes. Sometimes they even clean their shoes without reminding, and both of them now I notice, carry a nail-file in their pocket. But the real test is ears, and their ears are still a doubtful no-man's-land between child and adult. When I can take it for granted that their ears are reliably clean without my supervision, then I shall know they have left their childhood finally behind them. They will be men at last.

When children are very young they are acutely conscious of the slightest difference in each other's ages, but anyone who has once left school is to them a grown-up quite simply, and I think to young children all grown-ups are much the same age, except for the very old who come into a different category of beings. It is an outlook I can perfectly well understand, since I too think of society as middle-aged, with off-shoots either end of young or old. It is only that I have pushed up my ages a little from the children's categories, and my people begin their middle-age not on the day they leave school but round about thirty. I have always felt thirty not forty was the critical age, for to be young we must still be in sight of twenty-one I feel, and after thirty we are in sight no longer, we have turned the corner of a decade and twenty-one is lost behind us. From then on we are all together,

and I have never been very conscious of differences of age from
then till white hair and beards. I can seldom guess how old anyone is within ten years or so either way, and already Peter and
John are better at guessing than I am, so that William will ask
them rather than me about the ages of people we meet.

Another of our milestones is the dancing classes which Peter
and John now go to in the holidays as a kind of vacation homework. Dancing, they have decided, is one of the many skills that
society requires of them, like table-manners, or tennis, or making light chatter with strangers. They have set out to learn to
dance in the same reasonable matter-of-fact way that they would
learn to swim or ride or bicycle, for it seems never to have occurred to them that they might be embarrassed or self-conscious,
since it has never occurred to them either that dancing has anything to do with emotional encounters with the other sex. "Take
your partners for a waltz," says the dancing-teacher, and she
might just as well have said "Take your seats for supper." They
are just as unconcerned, strolling across the floor with their hands
in their pockets (I must tell them how rude that looks to their
partners), walking up quite simply to the girl they have chosen,
smiling and asking her to dance as they were told to.

The dance-room is large, with windows on three sides, and all
set wide open to the fresh air, because the dancers always get so
very hot as soon as they start to dance—so great is the effort of
concentration. Outside in the High Street the morning traffic is
noisily busy, the sunshine streams in, and there is a general healthy
bracing atmosphere of wholesomeness and exercise. This is no
dancing in a romantic setting of dim-lit ballrooms and gardens
as dreamy as backgrounds for Sylphides. But then this is not that
sort of dancing. Not that sort at all. To begin with they are all
dressed as if they were going ski-ing rather than dancing, in vivid
jerseys and bright wool stockings; and since their dancing is a
form of exercise rather than anything else, I dare say they are
right. The boys hold their partners at arm's length so that they

can watch their recalcitrant feet, they straddle their legs as if they were swinging an axe, they stride and bounce and bob about, and as for the music—it might not be playing for all the notice they take of the rhythm. It is all very vigorous and healthy and heavy-footed, and not at all as I remember from the days when I went dancing. For the music then was like a pulsing sea, drowning, engulfing, drawing me in from the bank where I swayed and hesitated and drifted towards a half-seen partner, was swept into the strong current of the surging water, with the dance steps only a half-conscious pattern of the irresistible rhythm.

But then the music at those sort of dances was not a scratchy gramophone, the windows were not bright with daylight, and we were not fourteen and fifteen but twenty-one. And fourteen, so it seems, is too soon for dancing, too soon anyway for boys. Some of the older girls do show glimmerings of understanding what it is all about: given proper partners they might sway and glide. But as for the boys, they are merely cheerful and energetic, and only feel at home in the Paul Jones. This, although they are too tactful to say so, is clearly the only dance they can see any sense in. The moment the music changes they grasp each other's hands with new enthusiasm, and charge and rush around in a circle like the hearty young hobble-de-hoys they are. So that one fears for the windows, and when the clasped hands break loose with the strain, the free end of the broken chain swings out helpless with speed, clattering against the chairs round the edge of the room, drunk and delighted with laughter and high spirits. But the music changes back to a waltz again only too soon, and they must go back to the tiresome business of learning the extraordinary steps and gyrations expected of people who dance. And for anyone watching, there is a delicious pleasure in seeing these innocents perform the movements and attitudes of dances designed for lascivious suggestion. Indeed I have never quite got over my surprise that society, generally so prudish about love-making in public, yet allows a young man to seek out an almost unknown girl, clasp her to himself in the attitudes of passion, and perform, body to body, voluptuous movements to voluptuous music, half-dressed in the half-dark.

Certainly these children would be astonished to hear that that is what dancing is about. They are like the choir-boy at Cambridge at Christmas, who reads aloud in the cool clear voice of innocence the passionate declamations of the Song of Songs. It is like swearing in a foreign language, it has no meaning, is simply a curiosity which we try out for our amusement. Dancing for these children is no more significant. The few of them who do feel the first stirrings of sex are rather hearty than voluptuous. They push and tease each other with cheerful goodwill, and no sense at all yet of the intense and secret withdrawal of passion. They seek each other out not so much because they attract each other as individuals but because they begin to share a new language, however halting yet and half-understood. And they are curiously awkward, as if they had grown inside them a new engine of which they are only half-conscious and do not at all know how to manage, so that they are driven suddenly and violently in directions they only half-intended, they are not at all sure what is happening.

Sex, I think, is not one of the things that parents can help with. It is too embarrassing for them to discuss it with us: we are too widely separated in its emotional sea—they merely paddling yet in the breakers on the shore, parents far out on the open ocean, and between us long stretches of wild water which they must find their own way through as we have done.

Nor is sex the only subject which parents should not discuss I think, unless they are invited. There are all sorts of things which our growing children may not choose to share with us. They are separate people now, and we are not after all, companions of their own choosing. There is no particular reason why our grown-up children should love us.

For the parents it is simple. Our children are our choice and our creation, and our attitude is an equal mixture of love and pride and pleasure. The very fact of being a parent turns us into a proud and pleased and loving animal. It is the natural and necessary arrangement for higher mammals, and everything we do for them in their long dependence reinforces our affection. It is why mothers must always be forgiven if they seem to consider their children as paragons, forgetting all the times they were tiresome or boring or sullen or merely dull. By the years of patience, and days of work, and nights of nursing, we have earned the right to be a little tiresome. Being proud of our children is an occupational disease of mothers, and we cannot help it.

Yet their very obligation to us might be a humiliating consideration for boys restless with dreams of freedom and independence, and gratitude is an emotion which seldom makes us fond of the people we are indebted to. We are not their choice and their creation as they are ours; it is as natural for them to be impatient to leave us as it is for us to wish to keep them.

Between mothers and teen-age sons especially, I can foresee all kinds of potential difficulties quite apart from the too-much-discussed ones. Although it seems not to trouble John and Peter yet, I should have thought it might be humiliating to be known in such domestic unromantic detail by a middle-aged woman. It would seem reasonable if they resented, now they are almost adults, my long-established nursery discipline. I must seem tiresomely dull with my household preoccupations, and dreary wet-blanket attitude to things like late-night jazz in the bedroom and smelly chemical experiments on the kitchen stove.

Yet so far we manage without quarrelling. Their attitude to me is a curious mixture, partly a childish habit of dependence, partly affectionate tolerance of an older generation. They regard me too with a certain amusement, because I am absent-minded, and because I ride my own hobby-horses with just the same enthusiasm as they do. There is also respect, not so much for my authority any longer, but for my judgment, for a degree of worldly knowledge and wisdom which still seems considerable to their innocent inexperience of the world beyond their own small lives. Yet they feel themselves cleverer already than a mother who can no longer help with their homework, and quite certainly they are stronger, taking over with casual ease the tasks of lifting and carrying which for me are a struggle. And I can see that it must be the greatest satisfaction to feel cleverer and stronger than one's parents: it must make up for all kinds of minor indignities. Perhaps it is the reason for their new attitude of protective patronage towards me, taking my arm, and carrying my baskets, and saying "Poor Dardy, you *do* look tired." I am delighted always, and if in the end they will like me perhaps as a person and not as a parent, that is what I should value above all else.

But there is a long way yet to go, plenty of time for storms ahead, and the likely difficulty, I can see already, will be how to control them without resentment, while they are still in our care. The domestic discipline is simple enough. They are reasonable creatures who see now that the household routine is not a code of arbitrary rules they must keep because I insist, but a worked-out compromise convenient to all of us. For as a family we do not live easily together: we are all too different and too energetic. Our household is precariously like four tops all spinning together in a confined space, it is only by steady tolerance and affection and considerable circumspection that we do not upset each other's spinning.

Many things the children once did as rules, they now respect as sensible family arrangements. They telephone still when they are late for supper, but from courtesy now, so that the rest of us shall not wait. They realize now that I must be a household tyrant, not because I enjoy it, but because I must bully them all to keep any order in the house against three inefficient undomestic men. If they resist or provoke me with too much arguing, I shall leave them to look after themselves, and they all know very well from experience how uncomfortable they are when I am not there.

They know however, how to manage me now. I can see them making allowances for my tired bad-temper, or choosing a benign moment to ask some favour, or accepting my well-deserved scolding with such rueful penitence that all my ill-feeling dissolves in laughter and affection. They know my moods even better than I do myself, recognizing with amused confidence every inflexion of urgency in my pronouncements. Sometimes a word is enough to send them hurrying off at my domestic bidding, but mostly they consider me the mildest and most predictable of despots.

"Peter," I say in a dreadful voice, "if you don't clear up your study this very minute I'll turn you out of the house to live on the pavement, and I'll send you out bread and water through the window on trays."

"Yes," Peter agrees with me cheerfully, "isn't the mess *frightful?* I *must* do something about it. I can scarcely get in through the door."

But in the morning the mess is still there untouched, the litter of papers and magazines and pencil-sharpenings, the pile of books long ago due at the library, the rags and polish and brushes for cleaning his Corps uniform, the untidy experiments long since done with and left to collect dust. And in the merciless morning sunlight I am suddenly overwhelmed by the squalor of a too-much-lived-in-house. I go and find Peter.

"You haven't cleared up your study."

It is not the words Peter recognizes as serious, but as a dog does, the tone of my voice.

"Oh dear, I'm sorry." He is penitent, but surprised at my vehemence. "Do you really want me to tidy it this minute? I will if you say, but I *really* haven't time before school. Why didn't you tell me last night?"

"I *did* tell you. I threatened you with all sorts of horrors if you didn't."

But I must sound myself again, for Peter takes my arm in the friendliest way, and talks to me in the sweetly reasonable voice they must both have heard from me hundreds of times.

"You didn't *really*, you know Dardy. Now *did* you? What you *really* said was that my study was disgusting (and I agree). That I must clear it out thoroughly (which I must). But that you didn't mean I must do it that minute—only sometime soon. And I reckoned I'd have to do it at the week-end before I went to see Margaret and Peter."

Which is just exactly what I had meant. On Sunday morning, I thought to myself, I would remind him really firmly, and insist on shelves cleared and drawers turned out and all sorts of litter down to the dustbin. It is only that this-morning with the sun shining in, it is more than I can bear. But Peter is too contrite and reasonable for me to insist.

"Well," I grumble, "can you just push the worst of it out of sight so that it doesn't upset me every time I open the door? And will you *really* do it on Sunday?"

So, nowadays, end most of our arguments, which in any case are increasingly rare. For it is time now that they managed without me as their nursemaid. If they forget things then they must do without them; if they are late for school they must be punished (but not, thank goodness, by me any longer). If they spend all their pocket-money on trifles, then they cannot have the new tennis racquet they wanted. They are old enough to choose for themselves.

It is not that they revolt, but that I can no longer be bothered. When they are young we must help them, for I think young children are like young trees, and must be firmly bound by authority to a supporting stake if they are to grow up straight and thriving. But it is very tiresome being the stake, for the discipline binds both ways, and the stake must hold steady always, while the tree flings about safely and irresponsibly in the winds of growing-up. To enforce any system of rules and discipline needs great patience and determination and self-control—of ourselves even more than the children. For we must stand firm, not only now and again when we feel like it, but steadily and all the time whether we feel like it or not. We must be as reliable as the law of gravity. We must sigh and be bored and accept the rôle of priggish parent. For young children are of too uncertain a balance to stand by themselves, and seldom wise enough to arrange their own self-discipline. Yet without it they are bored and unhappy, and I think we must help them.

Peter and John, thank goodness, no longer need me for this kind of disciplinary uprightness. They are perfectly well able now to stand alone. And I have noticed that the affairs they organize for themselves are always carried out with the strictest self-discipline and efficiency, as if they had merely to decide to do a thing and there could be no question of putting off or wasting time. They are far stricter with themselves than ever I was, and far less patient. Only sometimes do they weaken and sigh for the old irresponsible days of adult coercion.

"I decided that this morning I'd write all my birthday thank-you letters and get them finished with before I did anything else," said Peter. "And now I'm too lazy to start. *Do* come and bully me, Dardy. *Please* come and take all my books away and say I can't go out, and make me sit down and not get up again till I've finished every single letter."

But I am lazy too, and No, I can't be bothered, I tell him, and Peter agrees. "I don't blame you. It must be jolly boring making your children do things like that. Almost as bad as writing the letters."

It is very much worse, I assure him, as he will find out later on.

And so it is for anyone who is either kind-hearted or impatient.

As for how we are to control them in the things which still matter, that is a new and different problem now they are no longer children to be lectured, but thinking adults like ourselves. It is no use now our being detached and disapproving parents: they have their own point of view, as valid for them now as ours is. I think we can only influence them by being involved with them in their trouble, by making their problem our own. It is no use saying we are upset, or only seeming to be so. Such attitudes they despise and mistrust. If we are to sway them by moral and emotional pressure, we must first ourselves be moved: we must share their anxiety and worry and misery: not stand outside the problem as judges, aloof and detached, but take our part in their trouble as fellow human beings involved as closely and unhappily as they are themselves. We must suffer and be resolved together, for we cannot control them unless we love them.

Yet how exhausting it all is as we grow older, like the violent involvement of falling in love. By middle-age we get out of the habit of these emotional crises; we have grown used to the comfortable attitudes of tolerance and understanding and seeing things in proportion. But I think we cannot help troubled adolescents by what seems to them such sterile detachment. We must make the effort of sympathy, and share their trouble before they will listen to us, or can even understand what it is we are trying to tell them.

And perhaps whatever we do they must break away from us. Perhaps these last years of fair weather cannot last, and the boys' adolescence will soon be troubled by the storms we are always warned of. Which is only the more reason for enjoying this present lull of general sunshiny goodwill.

It is one of the peculiar luxuries of our modern culture that these boys who are biologically men should be kept as socially irresponsible as children, that we should shield them from all the serious business of living. For the teenagers we treat as children

were clearly intended for fathers and mothers, and their bouncing vitality is no doubt provided for the essential task of bringing up families. As tall as their parents and stronger, capable,
resourceful, powered by unfailing batteries of energy, we yet ask
of them physically and emotionally no more than we ask of children. It is a strange and delightful creation of our civilization,
this generation of cossetted young people as carefully protected
from adult life as flowers in a garden, watered and weeded and
sheltered from the wind. And because they were intended for the
rough life of the open fields outside, they thrive in this shelter
with exotic luxuriance. They are as vigorous as oat-fed horses
kept only for pleasure, and unchastened by the routine of ordinary drudgery. They have energy and to spare for dancing all
night or rowing boats furiously up and down rivers, and their
overflowing vitality is a form of conspicuous waste.

Yet in this luxury setting provided by the gardening labour of
careful parents, they are occupied with the very serious business
of what the caretaker downstairs calls "the boys' book-learning."
Their minds, I think, are deliberately driven to the furthest limit
they can reach, and if we keep them as children it is because the
adult state is too powerful a distraction from the life of the intellect.

In a half-conscious way modern society recognizes the luxury
quality of its young people. It takes an amused interest in the
goings-on of its teenagers, dresses them in special clothes, and
provides for them special games and music and publicity. Pretty
girls are news anywhere, everyone enjoys the larking of under-
graduates. We encourage them to live their irresponsible lives in
public for our amusement, lives as curious, if we look at them
objectively, as the lives of orchids in the greenhouses at Kew. It
is certainly odd to think of John and Peter, with their army boots
and farm-labourers' appetites, as a variety of exotic flower. But
that is what they are, and I shall enjoy it while I may. It is like
living with princes: princes not because they have conquered any

kingdom, but because we have never let them know there was any conquering to be done: they are natural aristocrats. And in this way of living where only their mind is taxed, their excess animal vitality bubbles over in fun and high spirits, carelessly and confidently.

"You mustn't mind us being larky at holiday breakfast-times," explained Peter, grinning and breathless from chasing John all over the house and rolling in brotherly battle on the kitchen floor. "It's only because we've got to let off some of our energy in the mornings."

No, I do not mind. It is what I am used to. But how much shall I mind, I wonder, when they have left us? Shall I enjoy my breakfast coffee in middle-aged decorum? Shall I like the house quiet and tidy, with no mess in the bathroom or litter in the bedrooms or smelly rowing-clothes brought home to wash? I wonder how much I shall miss them when they have gone. Will it leave dreadful yawning gaps in the household life? I suppose it must do, since we have lived together all these years. The house will be sad when they go. And I shall miss too the other worlds which I visit through them—occasions at school, and afternoons at the river, and their friends in and out of the house at weekends and holidays. I shall miss their gaiety and high spirits and unmoody companionship. And shall I ever go without them, I wonder, to the Natural History Museum? But perhaps there will be compensations too, I tell myself. I shall have time at last to do the things I want, and for my own life with William, so long now and so constantly interrupted. I shall be glad to escape some of the domesticity, for I was not born domestic but only made so, never really liking it in quite such large doses. I shall enjoy being irresponsible again, and feeling free at last of the nagging guilt that I have felt for years now whenever I look at the rows of helpful books on how to bring up children. I always meant to read them but never have. There has never seemed any time left

over from the actual bringing-up. I have skipped all my homework and now it is too late to worry. I shall go off round the
town instead, as the boys do after exams.

There will be time. Too much time perhaps, and the house too
quiet and empty. Yet I have always noticed—when people go
away, or when we leave the places we love, or something we
treasure goes out of our life—I have always noticed that before it
happens—this leaving, this parting—when we think about it beforehand we are overwhelmed with sadness at the loss to come.
How shall we fill our lives again we wonder, when so much is
taken from us? The loss will be a wound we feel, which will
trouble us always. We shall never be happy again as we have
been. This is what we shall miss, we think, looking at our lives
which will soon be so much poorer, and this and this. We realize
more vividly than ever before all the things we love: our very
pleasure becomes the most poignant of sorrows.

So we feel always before it happens.

But the most unbearable sense of loss, the worst homesickness
of all, so I have found, is this loss and sickness we feel beforehand, before we ever leave home. When once the break is made
our lives do not stay empty, other things come in and fill them.
We are too busy with new arrangements to feel as much as we
expected, or if we do suffer, it is only now and then fitfully, in
sudden waves of sadness, but not a sea which engulfs us all the
time as we expected. The sorrows we imagine are more profound and inconsolable than real life leaves us time for. There
are too many irrelevancies, and the simple sorrowful outline of
our imagination is blurred by all the indifferent trivia of living.
It is why, I suppose, our lives are so unheroic, poetry having no
place for the newspaper at breakfast, or casual meetings with
our friends.

So that this perhaps is the worst that will happen, this sense of
loss beforehand. When the children have gone there may even be

a certain relief, as there is when they go back to school. Besides there are years yet before they leave us, time for all kinds of pleasures together.

"Would you like to go and find William?" I ask them, "and tell him there's a new French film that I think we'd all enjoy."

"Splendid," says John. It is their latest word.

A NOTE ON THE AUTHOR

Nan Fairbrother was born in Coventry, England, in 1913, but spent most of her youth in Leeds. She attended the University of London on a State Scholarship and was graduated with honors in English. After trying a variety of jobs, she settled down to work in a London hospital, remaining there until the beginning of the war, when she married a doctor and became Mrs. William Mc-Kenzie. While her husband was serving in the R.A.F., she lived on a farm in Buckinghamshire, where she wrote her first book, AN ENGLISH YEAR, *which immediately won her a following. This following was increased by* MEN AND GARDENS, *a book for "anyone who wishes to be reminded of gardens even when they must stay indoors." She is the mother of two children and, as the present book makes captivatingly clear, now lives with her family in London.*

July 1960

The text of this book was set on the Linotype in
Janson, a recutting made direct from the type cast
from matrices long thought to have been made by
Anton Janson, a Dutchman who was a practising
type-founder in Leipzig during the years 1668–
1687. However, it has been conclusively demon-
strated that these types are actually the work of
Nicholas Kis (1650–1702), a Hungarian who learned
his trade most probably from the master Dutch
type-founder Dirk Voskens.

The type is an excellent example of the influential
and sturdy Dutch types that prevailed in England
prior to the development by William Caslon
(1692–1766) of his own incomparable designs,
which he evolved from these Dutch faces. The
Dutch in their turn had been influenced by Claude
Garamond (1510–1561) in France. The general
tone of the Janson, however, is darker than Garamond and has a sturdiness and substance quite different from its predecessors.

This book was composed, printed, and bound by
KINGSPORT PRESS, INC., Kingsport, Tennessee. Paper
manufactured by P. H. GLATFELTER CO., Spring
Grove, Pennsylvania. Typography and binding
based on designs by HARRY FORD.